C000111418

IT WASN'T ME:

Why Everyone Else Is to Blame and You're Not

Chris Addison

HODDER

First published in Great Britain in 2008 by Hodder & Stoughton
An Hachette Livre UK company

1

Copyright © Chris Addison 2008

The right of Chris Addison to be identified as the Author
of the Work has been asserted by him in accordance with
the Copyright, Designs and Patents Act 1988.

A CIP catalogue record for this title is available from the British Library

ISBN 978 0340 920718

Typeset in Esprit by Hewer Text UK Ltd, Edinburgh

Printed and bound by Clays Ltd, St Ives plc.

Hodder & Stoughton policy is to use papers that are natural,
renewable and recyclable products and made from wood grown in
sustainable forests. The logging and manufacturing processes are expected
to conform to the environmental regulations of the country of origin.

Hodder & Stoughton Ltd
338 Euston Road
London NW1 3BH

www.hodder.co.uk

For my parents, and for Daisy.
Entirely blameless, the lot of them.

CONTENTS

Introduction

INTRODUCTION

We're doomed. All doomed. There has never been a worse time to be alive. I mean, sure, we don't have smallpox any more, and most people can reasonably expect to live past their twenty-fifth birthday and all that. And, yes, there are fewer incidences of folk being trampled outside their own caves by mammoths, and we need no longer live in fear of attacks by 60-foot women, (that's true). Nonetheless, it's difficult to avoid the feeling that not only is life more stressful and unhappy than ever before, but the world is on the brink of some terrible catastrophe.

It's true. Look around you. The world is going to Hell. People may quibble about how exactly we're going to get there – in a handcart, in a hand basket, trussed up with gaffer tape and gagged with a squash ball in the back of a CIA plane – but Hell is where we're headed: standards have fallen;[1] old values count for nothing;[2] our streets

---

[1] No one has ever made clear what exactly these standards are, or from what point we are measuring the drop in them; however, we can be certain that standards *have* fallen because everyone seems to agree.

[2] Except for casual racism. That never goes out of fashion. That's a perennial British classic – like brogues and early heart attacks.

seethe with a mass of dispossessed youth who feel no connection with or affinity for SOCIETY or the use of consonants. The state of our national finances is such that currency speculation in cowrie shells is beginning to look attractive. Politics is peopled by pinched-faced career monkeys and Flashman-lite toffs who spend far too much of their time saying, 'Well, Jeremy . . .' and not enough reading *Running a Modern Western Democracy for Dummies*. No one feels safe any more. You can barely walk down the street without being globally warmed to death or exploded by a terrorist with a grievance, a poor grasp of most major gods' attitude towards wholesale slaughter and a chromosome missing. Our front doors used to be open and now they are shut.[3] We don't trust our neighbours because we don't know them, and if we did know them, we'd trust them less.

The world, as I say, is going to Hell. The question is, who bought the ticket? Sure, we could spend our time usefully trying to rectify the situation – involving ourselves more actively in politics, creating a sense of community in our neighbourhoods, secretly arming the police, that sort of thing – but these days *blame* is where it's at. If adverts for ambulance-chasing shysters on daytime television have taught us anything, it's that.[4] Because so many aspects of the modern world

[3] A fact that has decimated the paperweight industry.

[4] And if they've taught us anything else, it's that there are some really, *really* bad actors out there.

have – if you'll forgive the technical term – gone to cack, it is often difficult to locate precisely whom or what to blame. There are so many candidates – EUROPE, MULTINATIONALS, FAT PEOPLE, you name it. Everyone blames everyone else. THE RICH blame THE POOR and vice versa. Older generations are sure the young are the cause, while the young look at the older generations' history and cry foul. Doubtless you will be the same. In fact, the only thing of which you will be absolutely certain in this confusing melee of finger-pointing and mud-slinging is that none of it – absolutely none of it – is your fault.

That is why this book is for you. It is, in essence, the case against everyone else. Proof, as if you needed it, that pretty much all other members of our blighted species are, in some measure at least, to blame for the appalling state in which we find ourselves. After reading this book, you will know that you, and you alone, can look at yourself in the bathroom mirror and say, 'It wasn't me.'

Oh, and while you're there, you might as well squeeze that blackhead.

SOCIETY

One of the many questionable things to pass MRS THATCHER's lips during her inexplicable 408-year tenure as big cheese was her famous assertion that there is no such thing as Society. This is entirely wrong. To be fair to the old sociopath, it's near enough inevitable you'll end up with this impression if you live on Downing Street for long enough, as the only people you'll see out of your window are POLITICIANS and journalists. However, a glance at the census ought to have shaken her out of her error; it reveals almost by the end of page one that there are a number of people in this country from a number of backgrounds fulfilling a number of roles. In other words, there is Society. And this Society is *to blame.*

Gun crime, obesity, alcoholism, the adoption of hoods by teenagers in place of the more traditional battered top hat with the top bit bent upwards, and the apparently endemic compulsion to name infants Charabanc or Boswellox or whatever other fatuous noun occurs to the parents are but a few of the many things regularly laid at Society's door. And, to be honest, the fact that it has managed to summon the wherewithal to curate even this disappointing parade of unfortunate cackery is quite something when you consider how often Society is breaking down. You only have to open a newspaper to be convinced of this fact; Society's interminable breakdown is the second most oft reported in the world, after that of Amy Winehouse. Society is, to borrow one of the great irritating phrases of our times, not fit for purpose.

Now, why?

One of the great problems with Society is that it has been tremendously badly designed. Whoever thought it might be a good idea to have the poorer people as the majority and the richer as some sort of elite minority wants to take a long, hard look at themselves; it's a thoroughly idiotic state of affairs and has frankly caused nothing but fuss and bother since they brought it in. It's remarkable that they managed to get it through the planning committee at all. Common sense alone ought to have dictated that by far the greater number of people be rich – thus preventing a good deal of the social problems we face today, albeit at the expense of the crispy pancake industry – and only as many people be poor as are necessary to sustain daytime telly.

Society is also perhaps the ultimate example of the 'too many cooks' principle. At first glance, it seems a commendably inclusive organisation, numbering among its personnel absolutely everybody. This is nicely modern, extremely good for its public profile and plays well with the key ABC1 25–45 demographic, but it is apt to make the whole thing a little cumbersome and directionless. It is by no means certain that an IT consultant's worldview will be the same as that of, say, a milliner, or a steeplejack's the same as a pole dancer's, or a lawyer's the same as an actual proper person's, or a hippie's the same as an even more self-righteously judgemental hippie's. The fallout from this takes two main forms: firstly, a depressing number of highly tedious radio phone-in programmes in which idiots invite idiots to call and explain why they think other idiots are idiots; and secondly, Society appears to have no coherent standpoint on anything at all.

Part of the issue here is a very modern one. Present-day Society has no one from whom to take a steer on what to think; it is no longer clear who is in charge. In the old days, it was easy to tell who was in charge of Society because they were the ones on a horse chasing after you and your screaming, stumbling family and whirling a polo mallet. Later on, as you pressed your hard-earned ha'penny into a goat turd to hide it from marauding thieves and listened to the degraded grunts of the squire exercising his *droit de seigneur* on your womenfolk in the paddock, you had the comfort of knowing your place and enjoyed the accompanying abdication of responsibility. Nowadays, thanks to decades of misinterpreting egalitarianism as the right to ignore everyone else and the insistence of the political classes on carrying on with all the dignity of a Christmas party in a temping agency, Society is left without any real notion of whom to look to for its opinions. The only thing that remains from those former, more certain times that even approaches a reading from the collective moral compass is 'Thought for the Day' on the *Today* programme, and that is, in truth, little more than a signal to the nation to get in the shower.

Without leadership, Society has naturally turned in on itself and succumbed to internecine squabbling, to the point where it's difficult to see any sort of useful agreement being reached about anything at all without dropping the whole bally shower on to an island and coming back later to see who's still alive and holding the conch. The problem with this is that Society is already on an island and has been for some time now with no sign that anyone's found the conch, let alone kept hold of it. To be fair, though, some of us are a bit busy to go around looking for conches – that word search isn't going to solve itself.

There is a subsection of Society, however, whose job it is to provide at least the semblance of leadership and they are not doing it. Among other things, we call them POLITICIANS.

POLITICIANS

Here's an insight for you: life is incredibly complicated. It is, though, isn't it? It's all working out how to get the roof rack on and drawing up wedding seating plans that don't offend anyone and trying to understand ballet. Humans simply aren't wired for this kind of complexity. In evolutionary terms, it really isn't all that long since our distant ancestors stood up and walked out of the Great Rift Valley of East Africa in search of somewhere that was a bit less lion-y. It is a matter of mere millennia since the most sophisticated of our species were nomads – which is to say chased animals about for a living.[5] The limit of the intellectual challenge that our nomadic forebears faced on a daily basis was how to get the tent back in the bag. However, once we'd had one too many arguments about who'd left the peg hammer on the tundra again, we settled down in cities with a long-term view to inventing Center Parcs so that we wouldn't have to go camping again.

[5] An idea that they seem to have picked up from the lions they were so keen to see the back of, which just goes to show something or other.

From the moment that humans began to reside in one place, life became more complicated – the idea of property was developed, technology was invented, and there were the first thumping great set-tos about whose turn it was to take the bin out. Pretty soon we had to start parcelling out roles to make sure that everything got done. Some tended to the fields, some tended to the animals, some tended to the gods, and some tended to what used to be called shit-shovelling but is now usually referred to as the safe redistribution of unwanted faecal matter.[6]

Unfortunately, the very systems we devised to deal with the complexity of life have themselves become overly complex. Now, as well as the fields, animals, gods and faecal matter, we have to deal with transport, snacks, support hosiery, planning permission for gazebos and any number of other cogs in the machine. There are so many things that need covering in modern life and, as a consequence, so many roles needed to cover them that we've had to set up a system that allows us to deal with the complexities of the system that we set up to allow us to deal with complexities in the first place. Are you following this? It doesn't really matter. The point I'm limping towards is this: human SOCIETY makes the

[6] The way these roles were initially parcelled out was by means of games of Scissors, Paper, Stone. However, since neither scissors nor paper had been developed up to this point, the game became known as Stone. It took a very long time.

Gordian knot look like one of those puzzles you get in a Marks & Spencer Christmas cracker, and in order to function properly it needs a bunch of people at the top of it to oversee the whole thing. In other words, we need a government. This, and this alone, is the reason that we tolerate Politicians.

Now, there are obviously many reasons to dislike Politicians: the bad suits, the unironic use of 'Yyuryur' to indicate agreement, the evident pleasure they take in standing at the dispatch box forging clunking rejoinders from dull old bits of wit that would shame a local radio DJ. That they are not to be trusted is, as our American friends would say, a given. Those who currently sit on the leadership benches have that look in their eye that Arthur Fowler had just before he made off with the Christmas Club money, while the chief of the waxy snits who sit opposite has the perpetual air of a school captain who's just made an assignation with the French assistant. Smarmy, shifty and clearly the kind of people you'd try to lose in the pub early doors on a stag night (even if it were their own), Politicians are never going to be anyone's favourite substratum of SOCIETY.

However, where they really fall down is in the denial of the very complexity that makes them necessary in the first place. The standard MO of Politicians – and their greatest sin – is to try to make out that everything is simple. This is what so frustrates *Newsnight* presenters.

The reason Paxman looks as though he's about to leap out of his tubular metal chair and brain the Shadow Minister for Housing (and to my mind should be commended for his admirable restraint in thus far not doing so) is not, I suspect, due to the irksome lies and evasiveness of their verbal currency so much as their wilful refusal to admit that the age-old, intractable problems they find in their portfolio[7] cannot be solved at a stroke. Yes, you can try to staunch falling pass grades in language exams by making it acceptable for pupils to speak English with a French accent in GCSE orals. By all means make the NHS waiting lists shorter by printing them in a smaller font. Certainly, child poverty could be halved by reducing the age of majority to nine. Nevertheless, these are simple PR-led measures that fail to address the causes of the problems they pretend to solve.

Perhaps the classic example of oversimplification is the emphasis on interest rates,[8] which are talked about as though their manipulation is the key to the economy. It isn't. The key to the economy is like God: obscure, unknowable, not easy to draw and decreasing numbers of people believe that such a thing actually exists.[9]

---

[7] Along with some sandwiches, an apple and a clean pair of socks put in there each morning by their researcher.

[8] See THE BANK OF ENGLAND, p.43.

[9] Although, to trouble the metaphor further, those who do are becoming increasingly fundamentalist about their particular vision of what it is.

Politicians of course don't tell people that, preferring instead to maintain the fantasy that we have some sovereign control over our own national financial position and aren't – as is really the case – horribly dependent on the capricious workings of an international fiscal system so impossible to get your head round that it would wear out the battery on that little box that makes Stephen Hawking work.

Now, there are two possible motivations for this. Either Politicians are tremendously ingenuous and sincerely believe that matters are as simple as they make out – which would certainly account for their 'what-does-this-button-do?' approach to the machinery of government – or they are merely being cynical and assuming that the electorate don't want to be told that things are complicated because they are unsophisticated boobs who spend what little spare time they have sitting on their sofas and scooping Pot Noodle as close to their mouths as they can manage with their hands.

Whatever the reason, the result is that Politicians end up convincing the public, if only by sheer weight of repetition, that the world is as straightforward as they say and consequently find themselves in a position where it is electorally disastrous to admit that matters are, in fact, a little on the tricky side. Thus we end up in the vicious circle of stupidity that now passes for political debate and action in this country: Politicians continue to promise easy solutions that they can't possibly make good on; the public gets all narky and starts asking questions about where their easy solutions are in the form of opinion polls; the Politicians distract the public from the failure of their earlier easy solutions by putting forward different easy solutions and we all go round again. It's like a really rubbish square dance, and since square dances are pretty rubbish in the first place, I think we can all agree that that is one stinging metaphor.

Of course, Politicians are simply the inevitable products of the system that made them – the flawed piece of pie-in-the-sky nonsense sold to a gullible world by the bunch of sheet-wearing olive-guzzlers who coined the term DEMOCRACY.

DEMOCRACY

There are very few things in this life of which we can be absolutely certain. Death, taxation and, more recently, hosepipe bans are the three most often mentioned. As for moral certainties, there are even fewer in our modern world, now that fornication is considered less as a sin and more as a useful source of cardiovascular workout and that coveting your neighbour's possessions is pretty much the basis for Channel 4's midweek evening schedules.[10] In fact, only one such certainty remains today: Democracy is morally and philosophically the only right and fair system of government. The counterargument to this idea can be summed up in five well-chosen words: wrong, wrong, wrong, wrong, wrong.

Democracy is a disastrous steak tartare of a system

[10] Technically, of course, it's 'coveting your neighbour's ox', but that doesn't really fit with the way we live now. Although, if we did still live in a largely ox-based society, you can bet your three-up-two-down-former-miner's-cottage-with-great-views-of-the-fells-coming-in-at-ten-grand-under-budget-but-without-the-outside-space-that-this-week's-couple-are-keen-to-find that Channel 4 would by now be on to Series 18 of *Rumination, Rumination, Rumination*.

– mushy, undercooked and spoken about using words such as 'elegant' and 'sophisticated' where words such as 'horrifying' and 'basic' might do better. In this metaphor, leading the electorate into the voting booths and leading a cow into a Kenwood mixer produce roughly analogous results.

There is no doubt that Democracy is a good idea at the headline level. Giving everyone a say in how their country is governed sounds absolutely the thing so long as you don't make the mistake of examining that word 'everyone' too much. The problem with Democracy, you see, is that it is only ever as good as the electorate taking part in it. Great proponents of Democracy, such as older people and George W. Bush, imagine that every country operating such a system is full of grateful, shiny-eyed ordinary folk, skipping to the polling booth with a lump in their throat and their ballot paper in their hand, breathing their freedom deeply. Whereas, as any canvasser who's ever gone to get out the vote on election day will tell you, it's actually full of people who are 'A bit busy watching *Taggart* at the moment, mate, sorry.' It turns out that 'One Man, One Vote' may have been a bit of an overestimation of the level of interest. 'Two Men, One Vote' would have been more than enough to go round, and would quite frankly have saved a lot on printing costs, which could then have been spent on sweets or hummus.

Please don't get me wrong – of course everybody

wants Democracy, and many of those who don't have it are prepared to do quite brave and desperate things to achieve their goal. That guy in CHINA who stood in front of a bunch of tanks when the man on the pedestrian crossing was red, thus risking a jaywalking ticket, springs immediately to mind. Once we've got it, though, our attitude relaxes a little. Democracy, it seems, is like a gym membership – we're glad we have it, even feel a little smug that we do, but not that many of us can remember the last time we used it properly and really, so long as enough other people are using it to ensure the gym isn't going to shut down, we're happy in the knowledge that we'll probably get round to going just as soon as things calm down a bit at work and we've got Christmas out of the way and they stop charging 50p for towels. This isn't just the case in places where they've had Democracy so long that they can't remember what it's like being chased around by men with different ideologies and pointy sticks. In the 2004 Russian elections certain parties felt it necessary to entice people into the polling booths with promises of free haircuts, ironically making the country smarter and dumber at the same time.

In many ways, this disinterest is a good thing, because if you did manage to get the gormless sofa-lardies who normally wouldn't be bothered, to haul their squashy hulks the 300 yards down the road to the polling station at the local primary school, they'd only vote, which would probably be worse. 'People like blood sausage,' says the cantankerous weatherman Phil Connor in *Groundhog Day*. 'People are morons.' As misanthropic, unpleasant and self-satisfied as that position may be, it's not a bad principle. The same people who sit at the restaurant table next to yours and say in a flustered voice as the waiter approaches, 'D'y'know what, Carol, I can't work out whether to have the banoffee pie or the death by chocolate. I'm terrible with choice, me – I just *panic*!' are the same people who wander behind the little curtain with a voting slip and try to remember how to spell 'X'. And I'm not sure they're best placed to be making long-term decisions about our future.

However, for our purposes – apportioning blame for the State of the World – Democracy's major flaw is this: it allows people to perpetuate the notion that all points of view are equally valid. They are not. A good rule of thumb is this: if you have read around a subject, are largely conversant with current affairs, pause before speaking when asked a question and are not a member of a political party, then your opinion is most likely valid. If, instead of doing any of that, you barely wait for the other person to finish speaking before jumping in with a sentence that begins 'The thing is, Nicky, at the end of the day . . .' the chances are, your opinion is not valid. Unfortunately, Democracy is not sophisticated and it is not elegant and it does not demand that people participating in it arm themselves with anything so footling as facts, but it does give those people the sense that what they're saying is important and must be heard. This accounts for all radio phone-ins, the people who text in to the news, the entire editorial staff of the *Daily Mail*, that tit who's never out of your pub, student politics, the BNP, hippies, the *Loose Women* team and me from about the age of fourteen to the present day.

That said, perhaps we ought to be blaming the authors of the ill-thought-through notions that are bandied about, instead of those doing the bandying, because as often as not that latter group has simply got hold of someone else's maddeningly trite opinion. The usual conduit for this is their newspaper, which brings us to NEWS (PRINTED).

NEWS (PRINTED)

Fear, Man's old enemy, stalks the land like a . . . like a stork. Yes, like a stork. And the baby that stork is bringing is called Anger. And before you know it, Anger will be doing pre-school on the same two mornings a week as Hatred and having sleepovers at Insularity's house. And then how long will it be till it's stopping out all night drinking alcopops with Social Breakdown? Eh? We must ask ourselves, where has this terribly destructive Fear come from and is it justified?

Imagine a world in which the press did not exist. No newspapers at all. What do you think the most striking change would be? Obviously, public transport would be less littered and you'd have to take a book[11] with you on your journey to work instead of trying to keep yourself occupied with a discarded healthy-eating pull-out from the *Daily Express* featuring that Scottish bint with no lips and a poo obsession. Also, without those free papers that get walloped in your solar plexus

[11] An Andy McNab or a sports biography if you're a boy; something depressingly pastelly with faux-Parisian cartoons of shoes and chocolates on the front if you're a girl. I don't make the rules.

every morning by resentful-looking types in dayglo jackets it would be a lot harder to keep up with how Lily Allen is getting on, which would be a chore. However, the most significant change, I suspect, would be in our attitude towards the world.

Observed without a guide, the world is a wriggling sack of random events and facts, things that you happen to see as you go about your day – a group of overly exuberant but relatively harmless members of THE YOUTH OF TODAY congregating by a lamp-post here, a pleasant if introverted new Lithuanian neighbour there. It takes a newspaper to contextualise them and turn the first into an entire generation who make *A Clockwork Orange* look like *Why Don't You . . . ?* and the second into the biggest threat to British cultural identity since someone nicked the roof off Stonehenge.[12]

Newspapers connect the world for us. In principle, this is an excellent idea. In practice, however, it is somewhat spoiled by the fact that the journalists, editors and MEDIA MOGULS associated with those papers are, with a few heroic exceptions, a bunch of sensationalist, excitable, self-important, circulation-

[12] For centuries the fact that the ancients managed to manoeuvre the vast monoliths that make up Stonehenge all the way from Wales to Wiltshire has been used by a particular sort of person as evidence of the greatness of the Celtic civilisation that existed in these islands before the Roman Invasion. 'However did they do it?' they'll say, 'However did they get the stones all that way?' I'll tell you how they did it: look at a map. The A303 runs right by it. What's the big deal?

driven ne'er-do-wells whose ability to take on board and repeat facts accurately and correctly would be surpassed by a deaf man playing Chinese whispers in a steam museum. The way that we imagine the world to be is hugely dependent on what our paper of choice wants us to think, and whatever that may be, it certainly wants us to be annoyed or fearful enough to buy the paper again the next day so that we can confirm our suspicions that things are getting worse. The significance we ascribe that group of youths or that Lithuanian naturally depends on which paper we read.

If you read *The Times*, you'll see them as signs of the waning ability of POLITICIANS and policy to influence the make-up and values of the population they nominally represent. If you read the *Guardian*, you'll see them as voiceless victims of a country blighted by free-marketeering and the neglect of the public sector. If you read the *Telegraph*, you'll see them (along with absolutely everything else) as proof that the Conservative Party should never have hounded MRS THATCHER from office. If you read the *Independent*, you will see them as either contributing to or the inevitable result of global warming. If you read the *Sun*, you'll see them as something to skim over on your way to the football pages. If you read the *Mirror*, you'll also see them as something to skim over on your way to the football pages, but whatever that something is, it'll be the direct opposite of the something in the *Sun*. If you read the *Daily Star*, you'll spend far too long mouthing the words as you look at them to be able to form any sort of coherent sentence or opinion that you can then adopt and use in your life. If you read the *Daily Express*, you'll see them as possibly implicated in the death of the Princess of Wales. And then there's the *Daily Mail*.

Ah, the *Daily Mail*, the apotheosis of the fear-mongering newspaper. Selfishness and venality dressed up as moral outrage. If newspapers are supposed to be a window on the world, then the *Daily Mail* is like a window with the curtains closed and a man warning you to stay back while he peeks through them and describes to you what's going on in the kind of voice normally reserved for reading ghost stories to children. The version of the world posited by the *Daily Mail* is so terrifying that you wonder how any of its readers pluck up the courage to leave the house and walk down the road to the newsagent's to buy it in the first place. Once they've got hold of their copy, it must be pretty hard for them to read it through the red mist of fury and misanthropy clouding their everyday vision which prolonged exposure to the paper's views inevitably causes.

So if you read the *Daily Mail*, then you'll see the group of youths as a bunch of paedophiles[13] and the

[13] On the technically logical grounds that they fancy and have sex with other people of their age, and there is absolutely *no* excuse for that.

Lithuanian as a bogus asylum-seeker.[14] This is pretty much how *Daily Mail* readers divide up the world. In fact, the easiest way to confuse a *Daily Mail* reader is to tell them that asylum-seekers are the natural predators of paedophiles. It makes their heads explode, which, incidentally, is a good example of how you can sometimes give evolution a little leg-up.

In a way, though, it's unfair to blame the papers. Everybody knows pretty much what they'll get from each one and so they buy whichever most neatly fits their own views. The papers, for their part, make little pretence at impartiality. The television bulletins, however, are a different story. See NEWS (TELLY).

---

[14] Even though there's no such thing: you can seek asylum – that's your right – and then you're either granted it or you're not, according to your case. If there's such a thing as a 'bogus asylum-seeker', logically it would make people who apply for a job and don't get it 'bogus job-seekers'. The sponging bastards. How *bloody* dare they try and find better employment? It makes me sick.

NEWS (TELLY)

I am not a medical man – even my first-aid knowledge only stretches to the use of tourniquets and staunching pokers – but I am fairly confident that no longer shouting at the television news is a sign of clinical death. Complaining about the state of the medium has been a shibboleth of curmudgeons and furies practically since Logie Baird put down his screwdriver and said, 'There!' Lately, even balanced individuals with perfectly happy home lives must have found it all but impossible not to throw their dinner at the relentless cavalcade of idiocy slopped up nightly.

Over the last few years there has been a marked and depressing slide towards stupid, simplistic and, inevitably, downright insulting news presentation, most of which is predicated on the fear that if it isn't all whizz-bang and tinselly, we poor boobs will refuse to watch it. 'Never mind the body count,' they seem to be saying, 'check out the graphics.'

The epitome of this (though by no means the only culprit) is ITV's early evening bulletin, in which a big, tall man and a little, pretty lady stand inside a giant pretend clock and try to make out that this is a credible way to go about matters. They talk in the kind of tabloid-ese that merely belittles its readers when printed but which when used as spoken communication between one living creature and another sounds downright insane. This problem is exacerbated by the fact that they are only able to adopt two tones of voice. The first is the kind employed by overly patient care nurses breaking bad news to patients of impenetrable senility and deafness (so much so, in fact, that you half expect them to offer you a mug of cocoa at the end of the programme), which has the effect of making every single news story sound as though you had better make your peace with your loved ones, set your affairs in order and check the Book of Revelations for the evening's programme of events. The second tone, reserved for entertainment stories, is the kind of knowing, matey, verbal smirk that would aggravate the Dalai Lama into inviting you to step outside.

The programme's greatest and most worrying sin, however, is the astonishing propensity of those involved to editorialise. As a rule of thumb, I believe that the word 'evil' should only appear in news bulletins either in the reporting of direct quotes or with the word 'Knievel' immediately after it. It has no place in headlines. Perhaps they are using that and other qualifying adjectives to alleviate our busy schedules by making all our moral judgements for us, or perhaps they simply don't trust us to understand that car-bomb attacks in busy marketplaces are to be deplored. Either way, they're lucky we haven't marched up Gray's Inn Road to ITN with flaming torches and an indefatigable sense of righteousness.

The source of the problem is the belief held in many quarters of the television industry that programmes must be accessible to everyone. This in itself is not an entirely terrible idea, although it does often result in television the approximate consistency and charm of a stomach full of porridge. However, when combined with another, albeit unspoken, belief – that the public at large have the attention span and understanding of a particularly difficult toddler – it is deadly to news programming. The whole thing becomes a pantomime for the hard of thinking.

Correspondents 'interact' with fatuous computer-generated graphics for visual interest and open their reports as though they were pitching a novel to Dan Brown's publisher. ('This morning dawned like any other for the townsfolk of Todmorden, but only two miles away, a broken-hearted father-of-three had finally snapped . . .') Deskless anchorpersons stride about the place dwarfed by Brobdingnagian pictures of power players and villains so that we don't find the whole thing too static.

Worst of all, though, is the constant whining for us

to get in touch. Is there any more futile phrase in the language than 'Text us your views'? We don't have *time* for this. Seriously, the programmes aren't long enough to tell us what's happening in the world as it is, so the last thing we need is to waste time exploring Geoff from Grimsby's idiosyncratic take on the housing crisis. 'Text us your views' indeed. If you can adequately express your views on the crisis in the Middle East in under the 180-character maximum for a text message, I say you don't deserve a vote.

Over on what used to be referred to as the 'Other Side', things are little better. Many of the BBC's senior correspondents have succumbed to the unpleasant modern tendency of reporters to act all-knowing and wink-wink about everything instead of just telling us the bloody news. Nick Robinson, a man who at the best of times has the air of someone in the lower sixth who's awfully proud of the satirical magazine he's been putting together when bunking off games, will often open his reports with phrases like 'Oh dear, oh dear, oh dear, what a week it's been for Gordon Brown', which makes you sorely wish that the other members of the lower sixth would manhandle him into the CDT workshop and burst his head in a vice.

Television news is for the most part pretty much unwatchable for those not looking to release money from their life-assurance policy by means of a self-induced aneurism. There are honourable exceptions, but most of these are beginning to fray at the edges. I once – and this is entirely true – met an editor of *Newsnight* who told me that it was a fact that people could only be expected to process three facts in any one hour.[15] Luckily for me, that was the third thing she said. The point is, if someone in such a high position at one of the last bastions of decent news coverage is thinking that way, then it won't be long before they replace news bulletins with half an hour's worth of footage of something shiny spinning round.

What's so dangerous about this is that the failure of television news to keep us informed in an adult and reasonable way pushes people towards the press[16] (which is biased) or THE INTERNET (which is a big fat liar) to get their news. The long-term effect of that will be a population petrified into barricading them-selves into their houses with stockpiles of tins and a book of word searches until everything's better.

Perhaps, though, it's no good railing against the patronising dribble-heads who edit the news or the skin-stretched-over-ambition automata who read it; they, after all, are simply the point of delivery. The real founders of the feast of cack we're fed each night

---

[15] If this is true, then the whole examinations system needs an overhaul. Since the standard length of an exam at A level and above is three hours and a candidate will only find it possible to impart three facts in each hour, they can never score more than nine out of ten.

[16] See NEWS (PRINTED), p.16.

are the kingpins of the vast empires that set the tone for how news in all traditional forms reaches us, the MEDIA MOGULS.

MEDIA MOGULS

Ah, the general public. Bless their little hearts. They're quite sweet for a bunch of unthinking sheep with not a single notion of their own in their heads or any desire to get one. Occasionally, some sort of Polly Toynbee-ish Liberal blah-blah-blah pedlar like Jesus or MRS THATCHER tries to make out that people are individuals, but frankly the evidence is to the contrary. We've all seen the footage that usually accompanies news reports about public transport in which doors open down the whole length of a train and hurrying commuters spill out. What do they do? They all walk along in the same direction, not a single one of them fighting against the flow. Why? Well, to some degree they're influenced by where the ticket barriers happen to be situated, but mainly it's down to the flock mentality that is hard-wired into their ovine noodles. If you were some kind of power-mad lunatic with delusions of grandeur, a couple of newspapers and the right sort of vocal timbre for screaming at your secretary demanding they get the Prime Minister on the phone, then you might be inclined to see these directionless boobs as a means by which you could wield political influence. This is exactly how Media Moguls think.

There is a common misconception that we live in a DEMOCRACY. This is an easy mistake to make in a world where decrepit entertainers and their autocue-bound titty sidekicks nightly bellow at you to press red buttons and pick up phones and vote! vote! vote! to determine matters of such national importance as which celebrity hairdresser looks least like they're trying to kick their way out of a bin when attempting to execute a passable foxtrot. The fact is, though, that any time there is a vote that might actually count for something, the outcome is heavily dependent on the will of a handful of Media Moguls – men used to standing in rooms on the top floor of skyscrapers named after themselves, moving model satellite dishes around a giant map of the world and saying to their second-in-commands, 'Damn it all, Boxley, I want *Africa*!' These men are wily, they are resourceful, and their attempt to gain purchase with the politicos takes the form of a two-pronged attack.

The first prong is getting the general public on their side. This can be achieved only if that same general public willingly and voluntarily access the various media the moguls own, so to ensure this they employ an assortment of tactics. The news sections of their papers[17] concentrate on the kinds of stories preferred

[17] See NEWS (PRINTED), p.16.

by the desired readership: murders, anything to do with stealth taxes and the latest updates on which twenty-one-year-old from Essex with a 'k' in her name felt like going to a photo shoot in just her knickers yesterday. In these hyper-materialistic, sudoku-obsessed times, however, accessing news is very low down the list of reasons that people buy newspapers and so free gifts are employed to get them off the newsstands. These range from the opportunity to send off for DVDs of low-budget dramatisations of Barbara Taylor-Bradford novels, starring Christopher Cazenove and some woman you seem to remember from a chocolate commercial, to vouchers entitling the bearer to a seat aboard an aeroplane bound for Malaga packed with identikit slavering head-the-balls chanting 'Who Let the Dogs Out?' Once the general public are buying the papers, the Media Moguls are able to set about influencing them. This is done through a combination of headlines with exclamation marks, the matey phoneticisation of truly basic words and phrases ('wot', 'gotcha', 'Gordon Brahn', etc.) and relentless pro-robber-baron propaganda dressed up as populist common sense. Also, they tend to underline sentences in editorials to ensure that their slow-witted clientele **can find the point**.

Once the people are on side, there's just time to take a five-minute break for doing the crossword and buying all the available media in Asia before moving on to

Phase Two – bullying the POLITICIANS. Bullying POLITICIANS is a relatively simple pursuit, since beneath their carapace of arrogant but misguided self-belief there lurks the child at the front of the class with their hand up who is not sure if the cool kids like them. I have always seen the House of Commons as being not unlike an open-mic poetry night – blessed with the occasional repository of real talent and passion, but by and large made up of individuals who simply crave a public platform on which to stand while working through a few personal issues that might better be dealt with in either therapy or the pub. For no one is the craven desire for attention and popularity more extreme than prime ministers[18] and so, armed with circulation figures and a twinkle in their eye, Media Moguls are able to control pretty much everything a premier does. Again, various techniques are employed to this end, from the subtle (sending round mock-ups of front pages featuring the PM's head PhotoShopped on to Abi Titmuss's crotch accompanied by the headline 'Twat!') to the brutal (actually publishing a front page featuring the PM's head PhotoShopped on to Abi Titmuss's crotch accompanied by the headline 'Twat!') Inevitably, the

[18] With the possible exception of MRS THATCHER, who simply seemed to want to find a platform for telling as many people off as possible. If she hadn't become prime minister, there is every chance that she would have taken a leaf out of Ian Paisley's book and appointed herself as the head of a church she'd invented.

leaders of the land find themselves kicking about amongst the lint and the Murray Mint wrappers of the Media Moguls' pockets, learning to shape their policies and pronouncements accordingly, and thus it is that Media Moguls are responsible for the direction that the country takes.

In some small respect, this is a good thing: it prevents the POLITICIANS involved from having to think too hard. The latter are not terribly good at thinking, and when they do think, the results are usually not all that encouraging. Whenever you see newspaper articles referring to POLITICIANS as 'intellectually rigorous' or 'deep-thinking' or even 'learned' they tend to be pieces trying to contextualise some sociopathically lunatic diatribe by the likes of Enoch Powell, or someone more of the present day who's also given to hand gestures, going red in the face and trying not to say 'darkies'. However, there is a deep problem with allowing Media Moguls to be the ones calling the policy shots. Quite apart from the fact that it is hugely undemocratic,[19] there is the issue of whether or not they are any good at thinking themselves. They are most certainly canny businessmen, but that means nothing for their skills in other departments. Richard Branson is an industry leader and yet has still not got the hang of asking for a decent hairstyle at the barber. Conrad Black worked

---

[19] This is not necessarily a bad thing. See DEMOCRACY, p.11.

out how to make a lot of money but has so far not worked out what makes Big Danny, his cellmate, tick, which is why he never manages to keep hold of any snout or jazz mags for more than half an hour after the end of visiting time. Similarly, the insight that tits and bingo will persuade people to part with 20p on their way to the white-van wash of a morning does not necessarily imply a delicate appreciation of the ins and outs of Anglo-Arab relations or what ought to be done about the situation in Afghanistan. No wonder everything's going down the pan. The country is, to all intents and purposes, being run by a bunch of rich foreigners who don't even live here. And, if I understand my imperial history correctly, isn't that what *we're* supposed to do?[20]

There is a strong argument to be made, however, that since the Media Moguls' empires would be nothing without the coin and complicity of those who buy their inky filth and satellite whizz-bangery, the blame must lie with those by whose custom the empires stand. They bring it on themselves; *caveat emptor*, after all. And who are these *emptors*? Who buys the most newspapers? Who nails the most of those gauzy woks that can suck football coverage out of space on to the walls of their homes? Not to put too fine a point on it, it's THE POOR.

---

[20] See THE BRITISH EMPIRE, p.127.

THE POOR

As Edwin Starr might have said, 'The Poor,[21] what are they good for?' A fair question. This country is practically overrun by poor people – you see them all the time in Primark and on *The Bill* – and yet it's difficult to make out what they actually do (apart from stockpiling knickers and breaking down in interview rooms).

One thing that's as clear as an ornamental crystal-effect swan[22] is that they don't do nearly enough. As is well known, 95 per cent of Great Britain's wealth is owned by just 5 per cent of its population. That's an astonishing statistic. Think how good this country could be if the other 95 per cent of the population started pulling their weight. Forget the Chinese – they might outnumber us seventeen to one,[23] but we'd be all over them like a cheap rash. The Poor, however, don't seem to get this.

[21] 'Hwurgh! Good God!'
[22] Twenty quid down and then 200 weekly payments of a fiver. Can't say fairer.
[23] Although it's worth noting that per capita Great Britain has exactly the same population as China.

Worse, though, is that not only do they not contribute enough, but they actually take a disproportionate amount from the kitty. They place an intolerable strain on services. For example, the vast majority of people accessing the NHS are poor and yet not one of them works as a doctor. Not one. This is wholly typical of their 'take, take, take' mentality.

Is this a modern problem? Can the Poor of today be held to blame for the State of the World, or are they simply the inheritors of an ongoing, if slightly rubbish, tradition? There is certainly something in this – as the saying goes, 'The Poor will always be with us, except when we're at the opera.'[24] The difference, however, is that in former times they always had a definite role. Take the Middle Ages:[25] in those days before the advent of Dysons, the world was a good deal grimier and the Poor would obligingly wander about the place soaking up the ambient dirt like one of those static dusters for blinds you see in the Betterware catalogue. Then, between the Tudor and Edwardian periods, the Poor helpfully and efficiently spent their time cheering the monarch as they rode past and, in the latter years,

[24] I think that's right. You might have to check the exact phrasing – my Internet's been down for a couple of days.

[25] For the purposes of clarity, we are treating the Middle Ages as anything that happened before the time of Shakespeare but after the time of Asterix. As I say, my Internet's been down for a couple of days.

providing a living for social commentators. This long period of routine and certainty was finally brought to an end at the outbreak of the First World War, when the role of the Poor was very swiftly redefined as the thing standing between THE RICH and German heavy artillery.

Even at this point, the Poor of yore accepted the role that they had been given and played it out properly. While it seems astonishing that they didn't draw a line at being recast as trench-dwelling shell-shock victims unable to do much but tunelessly sing the first line to 'It's a Long Way to Tipperary' over and over again and walk blindly into hails of enemy fire, it is entirely in character. Indeed, if you were to make one criticism of Great Britain's poor people, it would be that they have never had the gumption to get it together to stage a revolution, and it's not like they haven't been given the opportunity. Remember the time that Henry VIII tried to give them even more of a numerical advantage than they already had by killing as many of THE RICH as he could through the medium of marriage? Nothing. Not a peep out of them. It's almost as though they don't want to help themselves. A point that is emphasised further by their basically admirable but ultimately wrong-headed attitude towards charity. It is well known that the Poor tend to give to charity far more than THE RICH. As you might imagine, this is one of the things that keeps them poor and thus, ironically, necessitates the existence of charity. If they just kept their money to themselves instead of constantly thinking of others, then a sort of charitable stasis would be achieved and we'd all be spared the gut-wrenching spectacle of *Children in Need* every bloody November.[26]

I digress. Since the days of MRS THATCHER, who all but tried to outlaw them, the Poor have lost any definite role. All they seem to do now is to wander around, contributing to the generally depressed feeling that we have about the place. They shuffle out to the chippie in their slippers, whey-faced in an old England top, and then shuffle back with a Rothmans in one hand and a saveloy in the other. They are, as my old granny would have said, just not making the best of themselves. Other countries have picturesque peasants – leathery, weather-beaten old soaks who wear faded waistcoats and hang around olive trees with donkeys, drinking cheap wine from an old gourd and cheerily hallooing passing tourists.[27] Happy poor people would do a tremendous amount of good for the mood of SOCIETY in general, as they would make the middle classes feel less guilty about spending the odd grand or so on an ornamental crystal-effect swan.

---

[26] And while we're at it, if *Children in Need* have raised so much for charity, how come they haven't fixed Pudsey Bear's eye yet? Where's all the money going, Wogan? Where's all the money going?

[27] Albeit you won't see them on Wednesday afternoons, Sundays or saints' days. This is down to the EU Working Time Directive.

To put the thin scrape of icing on the no-frills dough-nut, not only are the Poor an expensive, inefficient drain on the system, they're simply not even that good at being poor. In yet another example of Britain's dwindling skills base, the last ten years have seen a marked decline in the number of the Poor[28] and we as a country have been forced to look to New Europe to make up the shortfall in numbers. The cold fact is that although they might not say it, many people prefer this new wave of poor people because they turn up when they say they're going to and they have a much stronger work ethic. I may have mixed that up with something else, but you take the point.

Still, it's not like the Poor have made themselves poor. Perhaps we ought to be looking to the people who brought that about, THE RICH.

---

[28] That is to say, a marked decline in the number of people that the government are prepared to classify as the Poor.

THE RICH

Like most other people with a modern education and access to Sunday-evening telly, my knowledge of our nation's history is essentially drawn from high-end BBC costume dramas and what I can pick up from the £32,000-plus questions on *Who Wants to Be a Millionaire?* As I understand matters, between the mid-eighteenth and early twentieth centuries Great Britain was largely populated by Alison Steadman and Jim Carter, who spoke in restrained and elegant phrases to one another while young people straight out of drama school smouldered in breeches or bonnets nearby, wearing expressions indicating that the moment social mores relaxed enough, they'd be straight off to have a good old rummage about behind a tree. I only know three things for certain about that period of history. Firstly, no couple managed to get together without some terrible misunderstanding born of the manners of the time, causing a hiatus of anything between two months[29] and forty

---

[29] During which the would-be bridegroom would attend to his wounds

years.[30] Secondly, the Repeal of the Corn Laws took place in a) 1846, b) 1847, c) 1848 or d) 1849, and if you ask the audience, you're on a hiding to nothing. Thirdly, and most importantly, there was a better class of the Rich than the lot we've got now.

If the stories of such great writers as Jane 'Based on the Novel by' Austen are anything to go by, the Rich of yore leavened their particular brand of patrician acquisitiveness with a pleasing sense of social duty. Certainly, the majority of truly poor people lived in distressed wooden shacks on the edge of woodland and spent much of their time subsisting on corn husks and losing relatives at sea, but their squires always knew they were there and at the very least provided seasonal employment during harvest-time or chicken-strangling fortnight.[31] And should a villein happen to appear before the squire in his guise as local magistrate, then they would be treated as if by a stern but loving father and sent on their way chastened, morally improved

and his business in London until such time as he had a chance meeting with a mutual acquaintance that ironed out the misunderstanding and sent him flying back to the country to make an uncharacteristically emotional declaration to the would-be bride.

[30] Which would usually involve India in some way.

[31] One of many lost British traditions that have their origins in ancient country ways, much like Rosemarytide, the Fowlen Dance and Chabbledegable Day (pronounced 'Cholly Day') – the passing of each a tremendous loss to the colour and texture of our culture. I mean, I made those particular ones up, but the point still stands, I think.

but, most important of all, free to return to their cony traps and wooden milk beakers.

Of course, this is a highly simplified picture. Things took a turn for the worse in the nineteenth century with the introduction of the Rich: the Next Generation, often known as 'industrialists'. A group that consisted by and large of rapacious, unsentimental northern types, industrialists harnessed and refined the manufacturing processes of the Industrial Revolution in such a way that they produced vast quantities of both money and noxious fumes. These were split fairly and equally between the industrialists (money) and their workers (noxious fumes). Nevertheless, even these hard-faced, top-hatted proto-capitalists (usually Timothy West or David Suchet) had a social conscience of a sort, as some of the great social projects of the time can attest. The Lever brothers built their grateful workers the charming town of Port Sunlight, the Cadburys built Bourneville, and that nice Mr Scrooge built all those workhouses.[32]

These days, however, we are unfortunate enough to have a third generation of the Rich: 'Rich 3G', who don't actually farm or make anything, but sit in large glass buildings[33] bellowing into phones and massaging

[32] You may have to check this: the phone went while I was watching that episode.

[33] For the most part, this is the clutch of architecturally charmless structures that cluster about Canary Wharf, among them a building that one of my brother's friends entertainingly refers to as 'Thatcher's Cock'.

their genitals through holes they've cut in their trouser pockets. Since MRS THATCHER declared all industry illegal in the 1980s, the principal way of becoming rich has been to pass imaginary pieces of paper expressing ownership of small percentages of companies around the world by means of a system whose byzantine complexity is specifically designed to make an utterly meaningless waste of a life look impressive. The upshot of this is that Rich 3G, unlike the generations that came before them, have absolutely no contact whatsoever with what we might term 'people', except for the man they toss their car keys to in the executive garage. Perhaps inevitably, any social conscience they might have had has been eroded, weakening SOCIETY as a whole and placing a tremendous burden on THE POOR and the middle classes.

The best example of this is tax. The Rich, as you might imagine from their name, have a tremendous amount of money. They spend this money in absurd ways: on ludicrous cars, on slinky call girls, on hotels whose sole clientele would otherwise be people writing double-page features for in-flight magazines, on food no one else has heard of, on haute couture that gives them the look of a monkey who's been bested by a tablecloth. Most importantly of all, they spend it on accountants who work out how they can make it look like their earnings for the year fell under the personal allowance. This they do by exploiting little-known loopholes that allow them to claim everything they ever buy as a legitimate business expense,[34] from koi-carp sushi to Romanian orphans.

If the Rich actually paid the tax that they ought to, one of two things would happen: either the government would be able to cut everybody else's tax burden down to the point where spontaneous dancing in the street would occur for the first time since the Great Shoe Flea Epidemic of 1556 or there would be enough money in the Exchequer's coffers to pay for so many hospitals that the NHS might have to start looking abroad for patients, not just doctors. As things stand, though, the Rich's avoidance of what is due leaves us with a stressed, angry and fractious SOCIETY that is not furnished with the necessary number of hospitals to deal with the growing number of aneurisms and violence this is causing.

In essence, though, the Rich are simply the team playing at the more advantageous end of the one-in-three-incline playing field that is capitalism. Perhaps the parties who are really to blame here are the officers of that system, those whose job it is to keep the financial set-up just as it is. And as far as they go, the buck stops (once it has been changed into sterling at a slightly unfair rate of commission) with THE BANK OF ENGLAND.

---

[34] This is why it is not considered rude to ask a call girl for a receipt.

THE BANK OF ENGLAND

The best way to make your fortune is to invent something that absolutely everybody is going to feel they need but nobody has thought of yet: look at Bill Gates, who invented the computer, or that Chinese guy who invented the abacus.[35] I firmly believe that chest upon bejewelled chest of treasure awaits the man or person who develops a watch that can tell you not only the time, but the value of your house at any given moment – for, if what I can glean from the coverage of financial stories by the tabloids is on the button, the only two items of fiscal information that concern the people of this country are how much our homes are worth and how much it costs to fill a Mondeo.[36]

House prices have a tremendous influence on the nation's mood and self-confidence, which is a big old shame because there is nothing that they can do that will not be interpreted as, if not catastrophic in itself, at the very least likely to make the fortune of the guy

[35] Presumably.
[36] This particular economic yardstick has made more sense and seemed a good deal more relevant since Ford finally developed the Mondeo.

who invents the anti-faecal fan-protector. If house prices go down, this is a Terrible Thing as the place that you weren't planning to leave for the next fifteen years anyway is now theoretically worth less. Entirely reasonably, people get hugely upset about this, despite the fact that it has absolutely no practical effect on them whatsoever, because it makes them have to think of something else to crow about when the conversation turns a bit passive-aggressive at their next dinner party. If house prices rise, this is a Terrible Thing because it puts the double-fronted Georgian farmhouse that you saw in the *Daily Telegraph*'s property section yet another £2 million beyond what you could ever hope to earn in a lifetime, and that's got to be hard for anyone to take. If house prices neither fall nor rise, this is a Terrible Thing as it means that the economy is moribund and the whole bang shoot is likely to be snapped up by a cartel of RUSSIAN OLIGARCHS any minute.

An Englishman's home is his castle[37] and ever since 1086, when the lords and vassals of England tore the shrink wrap off their brand-new copies of the Domesday Book and started getting all prickly about how many virgates the cottars in the next demesne had, the ownership and valuation of property has had a great deal to do with the English sense of

---

[37] Although in fact very few have ropes round the beds or play host to fortnightly falconry displays.

self-worth. As Norman investors used to say, 'You can't go wrong with wattle and daub.' So it is only natural that house prices are part of the State of the World for which we are trying to find someone to blame. The question arises, who is at fault for whatever we're finding wrong with house prices this week? There are three possible answers to this: Kirsty and Phil, Sarah Beeny or the Bank of England. No one is going to want to blame Kirsty, Phil or Sarah Beeny, since pretty much everybody wants to sleep with at least one of them, so you have to hope it's the Bank of England. Fortunately, closer inspection quickly reveals that it is.

The Bank of England today is a mainly fictional body that exists largely for the purposes of appearing in period dramas and metaphors, and hanging around on the back of banknotes, promising to pay the bearer the sum of things. Besides this, it has basically one task: the setting of interest rates. As with house prices, there are essentially three things that can happen with interest rates:

1. The Bank can put them up. This is a Terrible Thing as, if the guy on the news has got his calculations straight, it means that the average family are going to have to pay £35 a month more, stretching their already overburdened finances as thin as unstirred Cup-a-Soup.

2. The Bank can lower them. This is a Terrible Thing as it sends inflation galloping, which, if the guy on the news has got his calculations straight, means that the average family will have to budget £35 a month more to account for hikes in the price of Marmite and Toilet Duck.

3. The Bank can leave them as they are. This is a Terrible Thing as, if the guy at the newsagent has got his calculations straight, the average family will spend £35 a month on consumer magazines in order to research the best remortgaging options in case the bank does something different next time.

Every single one of these decisions will result at the very least in a report by the BBC's economics editor on the BBC *News at Ten* telling us that the economy is at a crossroads (which she will film standing at a crossroads in an attempt to illustrate her point in the most fatuous way possible[38]) and at the very worst by the kind of flat-spin housing crisis that prompts the smart money to start investing in companies that manufacture either soup or kitchens.

In other words, the Bank of England enjoys a position unique to itself and Richard Littlejohn of never being able to be right no matter what. Whatever it

[38] See NEWS (TELLY), p.21.

does, it makes matters worse. So how, you might wonder, can it be to blame? If it is in this philosophical pickle,[39] it cannot be held responsible for its choices. To which I would reply, 'You haven't quite got the hang of laying blame, have you?'

In fact, the point is moot, since the amount of control over our economy that the Bank has these days is pretty negligible. Most of the fiscal influence wielded in this country, as all across the world, is in the hands of MULTINATIONALS.

---

[39] There have been many philosophical pickles over the ages, an Epicurean tradition established following Wittgenstein's famous complaint that he'd like to Russell up a Plato Bacon on the Hobbes, but there was nothing to put on it but salt and Popper.

MULTINATIONALS

Like any modern man of the world, I believe it good for my image to appear to have an interest in the stock market. To this end, I maintain a small portfolio of shares in companies that I like the sound of: Ashby-de-la-Zouch Corporate Raiders, Inc., Capitalism Ltd, and Uncle Smokey's Barbecue Chicken and Glue Shack GmbH being just three. Consequently, like any modern man of the world, I have a small brass stock ticker, which sits next to the kedgeree tureen in my dining room, allowing me to keep abreast of the markets while I butter my toast and marvel at the fact that the clumsy boobs who print the *Financial Times* seem to have spilt Ribena in the paper vat again. Not that long ago, the ticker would stutter out endless tongues of thin white tape displaying information about every tiny share movement in every tiny listed company. As I set about my devilled kidneys, I would be informed that Chertsey and Renfrew Tubes, Tube Heaven and Call4Tubes were down, while Castle Cylindricals, EverTube, and Harris Tubes and Conduits were on the up. Nowadays, the whole lot have been sharked up by InterTube and my stock ticker manages the occasional desultory clack as it reports on the performance of the decreasing number of massive conglomerate blobs that roll about the international marketplace absorbing one another. InterTube eventually gets bought by United Stuff, which in turn merges with General Things to form United Things, which (trading under the name Things! because someone from marketing decided it sounded more modern and less threatening) gradually swallows its sole remaining rival, AllCorp, to become AllThings!, which is eventually sold to CHINA. Now my stock ticker is quiet and I can eat my hash browns in peace and apply myself fully to colouring in the crossword.[40]

The rise of the Multinationals has been a Terrible Thing for the State of the World, on the whole. For a start, one of the primary causes of the modern feeling of disconnectedness from anything approaching a community is the oft-noted inexorable drift into dreary sameness that afflicts most modern town centres as big businesses clog up the high streets with shiny-fronted identi-stores. As you walk down the main drag of any small town of a Saturday, avoiding Friday evening's mis-aimed vomit by the black-and-gold municipal bins and wondering if the man with the faux-Victorian baked-potato wagon drives with the oven on, the same

---

[40] For sale: small brass stock ticker. Good condition. Little bit of kedgeree on the spindle. POA.

names, the same displays, the same fascias assault your vision. Nothing gives away the identity of the town in which you find yourself, except the evening-paper wallahs barking the incomprehensible syllables eroded by time that stand for the name of the paper they're selling whenever some fragile-looking old dear passes close enough to their stand.[41]

Identity gone, the sense that you are operating within your own community is erased, too. In days that might be described as being 'of yore', you would know that the money you used to pay the greengrocer would be used by him to pay the butcher, who in turn would use it for the call-out fee for the local pest exterminator, who'd come to look at the infestation in the meat locker that the butcher had been meaning to have seen to for months. The pest controller would use the money to fund his ongoing agreement with a gang of small boys to release the beetles they'd been breeding into the drains of key local businesses, and the boys would hand the money on to the local newsagent in payment for various illicit items of pornography. The newsagent, sick of looking at chocolate all day, would go and buy fruit from the greengrocer. You could be confident that whatever money you spent in the local community

[41] I have suspected for some years now that sellers of evening papers meet at a pre-arranged venue when their shifts are up to determine the victor of their daily 'who-can-make-old-ladies-drop-the-most-eggs?' competition.

would stay in the local community. Not any more. Now we know all too well, as we type our PIN into the handset, that the money we spend in our local community will be included in the profit of the parent company of any shop we use. This parent company is itself a subdivision of the European arm of an American-based Multinational, and in time, the little bit of money accruing from our purchase will go to an elderly man in New York, who'll put it towards gold-embossed bog roll for his house in the Hamptons.

Multinationals are, naturally enough, hate figures among the population at large, who see them as rapacious destroyers of tradition and quality of life. Why, then, don't ordinary people organise against them? Set up their own shops? Find alternative places to spend their money? For two reasons, mainly. Firstly, because it's been quite a tiring day and *X-Factor*'s on. Secondly, because the Multinationals have a secret weapon: hippies.

Hippies, or to give them their full name, bloody hippies, are quite the most thoroughly annoying subculture of our age. More aggravating even than teenage girls singing R & B badly at the back of a bus. They are the mosquito of politics. The march of the Multinationals has received no greater fillip than the incessant anti-globalisation protests that attend every major industrial summit, because just when it's most important that we attempt to curb the influence of these behemoths, the screaming, undergraduate loopers wearing rubbish George W. Bush masks and lying on the floor naked again to demonstrate something or other turn up on the news. They are, quite frankly, rather embarrassing, but theirs is the public face of the argument against the Multinationals and no one really wants to be associated with that. They do us all the disservice of making the Multinationals look like the measured, reasonable ones. So it is that these vast corporate concerns continue with their onslaught against individuality and community.

Still, it's all very well screaming about the Multinationals' lack of concern for the communities of our land, but in many ways you can hardly blame them: they are not really of this or any other country. There are, though, other business behemoths based closer to home who are cheerily reaping the rewards of the robber-baron way of doing business. They are the SUPERMARKETS.

SUPERMARKETS

Exhibit A: the minutes of a secret meeting of a small association calling itself the Bilberry Group, suspected to be a cartel of the leading supermarketeers. The meeting was held in the function room of a Little Chef[42] on the A14. Each of the attendees, most likely the headest of honchos in their own organisations, chose a pseudonym from a list that one of them swore he could remember as being the character list from *Reservoir Dogs*. This was done in part for reasons of secrecy and in part because otherwise there's little about being a glorified grocer that's actually cool. The meeting was referred to in all paperwork as 'the Express Lane' because it contained fewer than ten items.

Those present: Mrs Peacock (chairperson), Reverend Green, Colonel Mustard, Miss Scarlet, Mrs White. Meeting declared quorate.

Apologies for absence: Professor Plum. Reason given:

---

[42] Seriously, have you never been in one? They're amazing – all chandeliers and wood panelling and that. Not at all like the front bit of the Little Chef. Also, they do this Bottomless Flute thing where they refill your champagne for free if you order the Olympic Breakfast.

bought out in hostile takeover by Mrs White and gone to Belize with a bunch of Quaaludes and a whole stack of pornography until further notice.

Minutes of the last meeting: read and accepted once Colonel Mustard had insisted that immediately after the recording of his assertion that 'We've got all those little suckers by the balls now, yessir!' a footnote be added noting that the printed word is not very good at conveying tone of voice and that the sense of what he had said was not perhaps as harsh as it looked on paper.

Item 1: committee discussed milk prices. Mrs White suggested the cost of milk sourced from British farmers was still too high. Reverend Green noted that farmers were already at breaking point and unable to supply the volume of milk required for the sums currently being paid, let alone those Mrs White had in mind, without diluting the supply with the very salt tears of their shattered lives and broken dreams. Mrs White suggested that she would be all right with that. Miss Scarlet noted that she had already suggested such a technique to her suppliers but that it made the milk taste funny. Reverend Green asked her what she'd expected and hinted at the possibility that tears were not the bodily fluid her suppliers had used in the diluting process. Colonel Mustard said that he had experienced a similar problem and simply re-labelled the new milk as part of his Supermarket's 'Taste My

Finest' range, calling it 'Extra Creamy' on account of its slightly yellow colour. Discussion was suspended while Mrs Peacock took a call confirming the opening of another city-centre branch. Committee agreed to keep the matter under review.

Item 2: committee discussed the destruction of local businesses. Miss Scarlet noted that she had been distressed by the number of corner shops still operating and wondered what was continuing to entice people into establishments with such uncompetitive pricing. Colonel Mustard said it was sweets no one else had stocked since the 1970s and copies of *Readers' Wives*. Miss Scarlet said that whatever it was, she wanted to crush them underfoot like a 10p packet of pickled-onion flavour Space Invaders. Mrs Peacock opened the floor to suggestions as to how this might be achieved. Colonel Mustard suggested a three-for-two on Princes Meat Spread. Reverend Green suggested they ignore the corner shops and look to improving the quality and desirability of their own ranges. Mrs White noted that he should shut his fat, posh mouth if he didn't want an own-brand fist in it. Mrs Peacock called the meeting to order before temporarily suspending discussion while she took a call confirming the opening of another city-centre branch. Committee agreed to keep the matter under review.

Item 3: committee discussed issues of taxation. Mrs White noted that despite only turning profits in the region of £500 million, her company was still being taxed by the government. She requested suggestions from the assembled. Mrs Peacock noted that she had reduced her British tax bill to £75 by buying a small rock off the Scilly Isles and declaring herself a country. Miss Scarlet said that for tax purposes, her company was registered as a chimney sweep from Walthamstow with a sideline in large-scale retail. Colonel Mustard professed confusion and asked to be brought up to speed on what exactly taxation was. Reverend Green explained it to him. Colonel Mustard replied that he still didn't understand but that he was sure it couldn't be all that important. Discussion was suspended while Mrs Peacock took a call confirming the opening of an out-of-town hypermarket to act as an overflow for the one it was 50 yards away from. Committee agreed to keep the matter under review.

Item 4: committee reviewed the amount of land held in reserve by its members. Mrs Peacock stated that she had someone in her organisation whose job it was to scroll through Google Earth all day and negotiate the purchase of any green bits he might notice. So far he seemed to be doing quite well, she said. Mrs White said that she had won the better part of Scotland off Alex Salmond in a game of poker and that she was planning to roof it over as a Supermarket with the veg aisle down towards Jedburgh and the freezer cabinets up around Inverness. Reverend Green questioned how responsible holding on to vast areas of land was in light of the current housing shortage. Mrs Peacock noted that this was irrelevant as people didn't want to live in Supermarkets. Reverend Green noted that this was exactly his point. Mrs Peacock noted that there he went, then. Reverend Green was halfway through questioning Mrs Peacock's logic when discussion was temporarily suspended while she took a call confirming the successful expansion and refitting of the city-centre branches that had opened earlier. Committee agreed to keep the matter under review.

Once again, though, we may be blaming the suppliers of misery when we ought to be pointing the finger at those who buy it. After all, the Supermarkets would be nothing without CONSUMERS.

CONSUMERS

You're walking around a SUPERMARKET on a Saturday. The place is full of people who consider it appropriate to be seen out of the house in tracksuit bottoms[43] and middle-class matrons trying to squeeze the tops down on overfilled self-service olive pots. As you march through with your list, organised properly according to the geography of the shop, you glance in other people's trolleys and baskets – forty-eight boxes of PG Tips and a slab of butter in one; Horlicks, beef and toothpaste in another; a third with two bottles of Jägermeister and a pregnancy-test kit – and you think to yourself, Who *are* these people? I'll tell you who they are, my friend. They're Consumers, and they are the problem.

One of the great issues concerning the State of the World is the increasing corporatisation and enblandening of modern life. It is tempting to see this as the fault

---

[43] Most likely because walking up and down the aisles, trying to deal with the momentum and inertia issues thrown up by a trolley filled with 26 litres of Tizer and half of Somerset's worth of mild Cheddar every week is the closest they get to an exercise regime.

of corporations and, er, blandities, but much of the blame must rest with Consumers. Until the 1980s, Consumers were known as 'the public', but they were renamed by business and a Tory government to reflect their view of the people of this country as a vast, collective, gaping maw, blindly guzzling all before it and producing nothing.[44] This was, of course, depressingly offensive, but unfortunately people have a habit of turning out like the name they've been given suggests they will,[45] and much the same thing has happened to Consumers.

'Give the people what they want,' runs the maxim. What the people want is everything, and they want it now, and they want it cheaply, and, if applicable, with free SuperSaver delivery on orders over £15. Let us, as though we were James Brown, break this thing down.

They want everything. Everything, naturally enough, comes from everywhere. In lorries, on planes and very

[44] Before judging the Tories too harshly for this more-than-usually distasteful and arrogant instance of greed-driven misanthropy, it's worth reflecting on the fact that it got them returned to power three times in a row. Well, that and the fact that most people wanted to see how far MRS THATCHER could get before the Queen said, 'Right!' and started rolling up her sleeves as she stomped down the dais at the State Opening of Parliament.

[45] You know the sort of thing: Sharons end up being giggly, Margarets formidable, Winstons reasonably self-confident, Evels quite good at motorcycling and Kofis disappointed at the intransigence of American delegations.

occasionally by post. The first two of these have a huge impact on global warming, and although post doesn't – since instead of using conventional transport, the postal system employs a series of enormous underground metal communication tubes, the ends of which are painted red and poke out of the pavement[46] – there is a considerable carbon footprint created by the amount of CO_2 produced by posties' cheery whistling as they go about their rounds.

They want it now. In order to have everything you want at once, you have to ignore certain footling, old-fashioned inconveniences such as the laws of nature and where the Earth happens to be in relation to the Sun at any given moment. Where once we had seasons, the furious certainty of Consumers that it is their right to have strawberries in December[47] has led to a world in which the only real way to distinguish one sort of SUPERMARKET fruit from another in a blind tasting would be to ask someone without a blindfold to tell you what you're eating. Significantly, SUPERMARKETS are at the very forefront of funding scientific research into anti-gravity technology. This is due to the fact that they want to find a better way of transporting their

---

[46] I expect they were designed by Isambard Kingdom Brunel. That sort of thing usually is.

[47] As with so many other rights, should you query whence this one derives it will be explained to you in no uncertain terms that we won the war.

fruit, most of which seems only to be held together by surface tension, without so much of it simply bursting en route.

They want it cheaply. You only have to witness the phalanx of squealing horrors galumphing their way through the doors as they open for the Primark sale, whirling a ramekin in a sock to give them that extra advantage, to realise quite how highly Consumers value cheapness.[48] This is why so much of the food they buy contains meat that is 'mechanically recovered'. What a lovely idea that is: meat so hard to get at and so beyond the fingernails of humans that a machine has had to be invented to melt it off the carcass. Mmm. *Bon appétit.* To disguise the fact that this presumably tastes like the animal's gut boiled in its own soul, enormous amounts of salt are added to the finished slop. Consumers' taste buds get used to this and eventually the focus groups that filter what new products make it to the shelves become incapable of recommending anything that doesn't taste like the bottom of a bag of Salt 'n' Shake crisps. Before you know it, SUPERMARKETS are only selling things that taste of the sea or of nothing.

All that said, perhaps it is a little harsh to lump all Consumers in together. After all, there is one subset

---

[48] The same is true at the Harrods sale, of course; it's just that there the Consumers tend to have someone to do the sock-whirling for them.

of that group who contribute disproportionately to the coffers of the SUPERMARKETS. I think we all know who that is. Don't we, FAT PEOPLE?

FAT PEOPLE

Great Britain. Think about that phrase: Great Britain. Is it really *Great* Britain? I mean, yes, obviously, technically it is. In fact, really it's the United Kingdom of Great Britain and Northern Ireland, but most of us call it Great Britain. Well, OK, fine, some of us might call it the United Kingdom or the UK or even . . . Never mind. My point is, is it any good? Or great, rather? And if not, why not? Looking at the Great Britain (or United Kingdom or UK or whatever) of today, we see the tattered remnants of a once-magnificent welfare state flapping in the breeze like bingo wings at a Cliff Richard concert, bankrupted almost out of existence by that great peril, that scourge of our times: Fat People.

The British government have spent the last couple of years getting very exercised indeed about Fat People.[49] Barely a month goes by without a junior politico from the Department of Health (or the Ministry of Wellness or the Hardihood Office or whatever asinine nomenclature it's been ascribed this week

[49] Which is ironic, for obvious reasons.

in an attempt to make us forget that it's been rubbish for years) being trotted on to *Newsnight* to sit in front of Gavin Esler and breathlessly saying, 'The fatties are coming! The fatties are coming!' Of course, they don't use quite those words, but they might as well. At first glance, what they're telling us doesn't seem much cause for worry. So the fatties are coming. So what? We'll see them miles off – they're huge. We'll simply surround ourselves with chip vans and they'll never penetrate the defences. And in any case, what's wrong with fat people? We *need* fat people. They're our only chance if the Chinese do ever decide to jump up and down at the same time. As soon as we see that tidal wave, it's 'Up you go, fatties!' We send one back and the whole thing cancels out around Chicago. It makes perfect military sense.

However, if you look into it further, you begin to see how right those government officials are. A report made to the Department of Health in 2006 stated that not only are these people and their lifestyles an astonishing burden on the NHS, but if things continue as they are, spending on the NHS will increase by £30 billion over the next twenty years.[50] And that's not to mention the amount of licence payers' money that will be spent by BBC news teams going round shooting those weird images of appar-

---

[50] The report does not explicitly state how much of that money will be spent on healthcare and how much on shoring up building structures, but fifty-fifty's probably a fair guess.

ently headless fat people walking down the high street that they always use to accompany reports on the obesity epidemic.[51]

You don't have to look at official statistics to see the scale of the problem. Hang around a school long enough and you'll see it.[52] Time was that there was one fat kid in each class. This was only right and proper, as every class team needs a goalie. Nowadays, though, the situation is practically reversed, presumably thanks to quota culture and positive discrimination. This is yet another tragic example of political correctness making matters worse by being sympathetic about a problem instead of tackling it head on. Fat People (and we can't even call them that these days: thanks to the PC brigade, we have to refer to them as 'People Whose Food Is All Beige') are given sympathy, which is a wholly counterproductive idea. After all, what comes with sympathy? Tea. And what comes with tea? Biscuits. Exactly. The whole thing plays right into their hands. It's almost as though that's what they were after all along.

The appalling truth of the matter is that the

[51] In fairness, the reason that the cameramen are instructed not to film fat people's heads is that they'd have to be pixellated before they could be shown on the telly, and to be honest, that's a lot of pixels. Believe me, pixels don't come cheap.

[52] If you *are* planning to hang around a school, it's probably best to wear a fluorescent jacket and carry one of those big 'Children Crossing' sticks. People get a bit antsy otherwise.

irresponsible strain on public services caused by Fat People[53] is simply the tip of the iceberg. These people's lifestyles have contributed to pretty much every modern problem you care to name. A few random examples: if it weren't for the amount of overeating being done, we wouldn't have to import quite so much food, which would both slash our national carbon footprint (global warming) and mean fewer lorries coming into the country for illegal IMMIGRANTS to cling on to the bottom of (immigration). The booming market in spinnaker-scaled garments to clothe this monstrous shower has meant a sharp increase in the number of stitches per capita and therefore in the amount of sewing time required to maintain the nation's clothing supply as a whole. This has had a catastrophic impact on working conditions in Oriental sweatshops, where tea breaks have been slashed by anything up to a half (child labour). I haven't quite worked out a link from Fat People to Islamic extremism yet, but I bet it's there if you look for it. It's probably got something to do with baklava.

See, it's all too easy to be taken in by the outward jolliness of a Roy Kinnear or a Luciano Pavarotti. Yes, Fat People always seem friendly; yes, they're good to have around when you need someone to dress up as

---

[53] And it isn't just the NHS, it's everything. Right down to public transport, even. How do you think those buses got bendy in the first place?

Santa at work; yes, Buddha was one. But they are eroding our nation, and not just literally.

There is something to be said for the idea that obesity is a modern affliction. There were very few fat cavemen. That is in some measure to do with diet and the amount of physical activity they would undertake, but it is also because fat cavemen would have been easier to spot and pretty slow off the mark, making them a tasty and effortlessly won snack for any passing pterodactyls. Ironically, though, the present generations of fatties are the result of a more frenetic lifestyle than that of our forebears, since most often they have reached their gargantuan status through comfort-eating precipitated by THE RELENTLESS PACE OF MODERN LIFE.

THE RELENTLESS PACE
OF MODERN LIFE

You're reading this on the loo, right? Of course you are. I knew you would be. We nearly put a perforated line across the inside of each page to make them easier to tear out in an emergency.[54] Why? Well, partly it's because it's that kind of book and partly it's because you've already finished the edition of *Puzzler* you've had hanging around for three months, but mainly it's because the time spent attending to what I like to refer to, for the sake of propriety, as your 'basement ablutions' are more or less the only chance you have to pick up a book these days.

The Relentless Pace of Modern Life is one of the key factors eroding the spiritual and social well-being of SOCIETY. We have no time for each other any more. Thanks to an unhappy marriage of technology, materialism, ambition and endless magazine articles by people who are prepared to play on the paranoia of

[54] Oh, don't be so coy. We've all been there. I still don't know how *The Da Vinci Code* ends. Mind you, I must confess that on that occasion I hadn't actually run out of paper.

their readers by pretending to know what everyone else is up to, most of us now live at such a speed that if we ever were to find ourselves in the kind of potentially fatal situation where our life flashed before our eyes, the resulting strobe effect could very possibly bring on an epileptic fit. Precious little stopping and smelling of roses is being done these days. Not even by those people who sell them to couples in pubs, and they've actually got roses to smell right there in front of them in an unpleasant-looking bucket. That's how bad things have got.[55]

There really isn't a minute spare in anyone's day. The following is typical:

6.30 a.m. Alarm goes. Jump out of bed in kung-fu stance.

6.31 a.m. Scratch gonads.

6.32 a.m. Feel guilty about time wasted scratching gonads instead of furthering career. Check BlackBerry out of guilt. No symbols indicating anyone has rung or emailed.

6.33 a.m. Switch BlackBerry on and off in case there has been some malfunction. Still no symbols. Ring answering service just to double-check. No messages. Wonder if this is a bad sign. Resolve to make the early train so as to be in office before boss.

6.34 a.m. Get in shower. Make mental note while

---

[55] Or, if you're reading this book in America, that's how bad things have gotten.

cleaning gonads that scratching gonads and cleaning gonads could in future be done at same time. Feel pleased at own grasp of time-management principles and promise self extra Berocca vitamin supplement as reward.

6.40 a.m. Get dressed. Feel annoyed about wasting the two minutes this takes. Wonder if that machine Gromit used for getting Wallace dressed in the morning is commercially available. Make mental note to Google it from BlackBerry on train.

6.42 a.m. Eat power bar and energy gel on way downstairs. Drink latte which was made last night to save time and left on shelf above hall radiator to keep warm.

6.44 a.m. Finish gagging.

6.45 a.m. Pick up BlackBerry, mobile phone, iPod, laptop, pen drive, portable DVD player, wireless dongle, Bluetooth headset, Kenwood Smoothie Master and leave house.

6.47 a.m. Return to house with Kenwood Smoothie Master. Dock self extra Berocca.

6.48 a.m. Leave house again. Resolve to yomp to station to make up time, despite not really knowing what yomping is but recalling that it seemed very important and impressive around the time of the Falklands conflict.

7.10 a.m. Arrive on platform. Hear one fellow passenger say to another, 'Why is that guy skipping?' Stop yomping. Check electronic sign. Note that train is seven minutes late and made up of four fewer coaches than usual. Vent frustration by doing press-ups against empty bench.

7.11 a.m. Ask man at cappuccino kiosk if he has towel for wiping paint off hands.

7.20 a.m. Train arrives. Discard towel. Choose *Seven Habits of Highly Effective People* audiobook on iPod. Locate point of least resistance in rammed doorway of crowded train. Crush old lady against woman with Next power suit and Marian Keyes novel. Proceed to look at ceiling for rest of journey.

7.55 a.m. Reach office. Hide in bush for a moment and put 'The Final Countdown' by Europe on iPod.

7.59 a.m. Jump out of bush, roar at sky and swan into office like the big 'I Am'.

8 a.m. Reach desk. Look around ostentatiously and say, 'The doctor is in!' before sitting down and checking BlackBerry again. Still nothing.

8.01–10.30 a.m. Pretend to understand job.

10.30 a.m. Berocca break. Smack lips and say, 'Yeeeeeeeah, that's what I'm talking about.'

10.31 a.m.–1 p.m. Pretend to understand job.

1–2 p.m. Eat various superfoods at desk as determined by whatever badly researched article was in colour supplement at weekend. Talk loudly on phone with friend about possibility of snowboarding weekend next month. Volunteer to do research. Spend rest of lunch hour looking at price-comparison-site comparison sites to determine which price-comparison site to use to determine which site to use to book snowboarding weekend. Run out of lunch hour. Check BlackBerry. Still nothing.

2–3.41 p.m. Pretend to understand job.

3.42 p.m. Phone Mother knowing she will be out at Makro bulk-buying for church coffee morning. Leave message on her phone asking her to return call. Give her number of BlackBerry.

3.43–4.26 p.m. Pretend to understand job.

4.27 p.m. Check BlackBerry. Still nothing. Phone Mother to make sure she's still out. Mother answers phone and says she was about to call. Lie about being called away by boss and ask Mother to phone back shortly.

4.28–4.58 p.m. Pretend to understand job.

4.59 p.m. Check BlackBerry. Still nothing.

5 p.m. Pack up BlackBerry, mobile phone, iPod, laptop, pen drive, portable DVD player, wireless dongle, Bluetooth headset, Casio Desktop Shred-o-Matic and leave office.

5.02 p.m. Return to office with Casio Desktop Shred-o-Matic, keeping eyes lowered as pass colleagues leaving for the day.

5.03 p.m. BlackBerry rings. Look about to see an empty office. Screen says, 'Mum.' Press 'busy'. Go to gym.

5.30 p.m. Emerge from changing rooms at gym to see bunch of muscle Marys bench-pressing each other.

5.32 p.m. Pretend to increase resistance on exercise bike. Proceed to spend next forty-five minutes watching the telly showing VH1 on off-chance they play that Kylie video where you can almost see her arse.

6.17 p.m. Get off bike. Watch someone doing warm-down exercises. Try to copy them.

6.18 p.m. Limp to steam room.

6.45 p.m. Leave steam room.

7.15 p.m. Give up trying to make face less pink with cold water.

7.35 p.m. Board homeward train. Ignore evils from woman with Next power suit and Marian Keyes novel. Choose *Who Moved My Cheese?* audiobook on iPod. Mouth along.

8.25 p.m. Arrive home. Find broken Kenwood Smoothie Master in hallway with Post-it from cleaner saying, 'This was behind the door – sorry!'

8.27 p.m. Eat power bar and energy gel on way to lounge.

8.28 p.m. Get laptop out and spend next couple of hours on Facebook updating profile, adding applications and trying to find the girl who sat in front in maths.

11.56 p.m. Wake in front of *The Sky at Night*.

11.58 p.m. Head upstairs to bed. Scratch gonads. Remember time-management idea from earlier and get annoyed with self for not remembering before scratching gonads.

12.01 a.m. Place two sheets of Kleenex and a tube of heavy-duty moisturiser by bed in case of problems sleeping. Turn light out.

12.02 a.m. Turn light back on.

12.04 a.m. Bin tissues. Fall asleep.

It's when we compare this scenario to the equivalent one for people from a bygone time that we see quite how relentless the Relentless Pace of Modern Life truly is. This would have been the typical day in the thirteenth century:

Just before dawn. Rise and walk to feudal lord's field.

Dawn–nightfall. Till feudal lord's field.

After nightfall. Till own pathetic plot. Sit staring at family in the fading embers. Die of Black Death (optional).

Simpler, happier days, I think we can all see. Mind you, even the 1980s were pretty relaxing compared to how we've got it these days. The only people who ever used to get het up back then were those men who you used to see on the news, packed into the stock market, gesticulating wildly and screaming at anyone who would listen and either dying of an embolism or a Porsche crash. In the last ten years, though, everything has changed, thanks to our new-found ability to be in contact with everyone and everything at all times. The blame for this handbrake turn of a cultural shift must lie with Al Gore's second most famous invention after global warming: that nexus of half-truths and amateur gynaecology that is THE INTERNET.

THE INTERNET

It is a depressing truth that the impetus for the technological progress behind many of the modern conveniences
we take for granted has been pornography, that least
reputable of all the '-ographies'.[56] Photography, video and
kidney dialysis machines[57] have all benefited from
mankind's insatiable desire to see photocopier-repair men
making unlikely, spontaneous love to bored secretaries
while a man just out of shot vamps on a synthesiser.
Such is the case with the Internet. The single reason
that the Internet succeeded was because Ceefax is too
blocky for porn. It would be very difficult, for example,
to tell whether you were looking at mainland Britain
and the Isle of Wight on the weather map or some
woman flinging ping-pong balls about with her pelvic
floor. It is hardly surprising, then, given the Internet's
foundations are shored up by the virtual-skin trade, that
it is largely to blame for the degradation of culture and
attitudes in our world. It has affected everything.

[56] Although it is given a run for its money by tossography, which is
the art of writing articles on Wikipedia.
[57] You do *not* want to know.

Education

It has long been traditional to blame the education system for the unacceptable levels of illiteracy and grammarlessness in this country. This is at worst a scandalous misrepresentation, and at best a fundamental misunderstanding of how easy or otherwise it is to explain the function of the indirect object of a sentence while simultaneously batting off a flick knife with a window pole. In truth, it is the Internet that is to blame. Since it is a fact – not a proven fact, but a fact nonetheless – that all children spend every spare moment they can gawping at the Internet between the ages of three and whenever they end up being hospitalised because the skin on their backsides has knitted itself into the fabric of their desk chair, we cannot underestimate its influence. It seems to have convinced millions upon millions of people, some of them old enough to know better, that a semicolon's main purpose is to look a bit like a wink if you tilt your head 90 degrees. A brief survey of your email in-box should be all that's needed to convince you of the imminent extinction of capital letters. You remember capital letters – big fellas, used to hang around at the beginning of sentences and proper nouns. Well, no longer. Capital letters have been sent off to hang out in the day room of the Home for Abandoned Punctuation, reminiscing with all the commas and apostrophes about what life

77

was like back when lard-wits didn't write, 'Lol!!!!' at the end of every sentence. Well done, the Internet, thnx 4 that ;-)

Economy

There is, you'll doubtless be tired of hearing, a pensions crisis in this country. Most people are failing to save for the future. Now, why? I'll tell you why, friend: one-click ordering, that's why. Yet another of the ways in which Capitalism, Inc. has turned the Internet to its advantage. Any system in which you can find yourself, a couple of days after having a few glasses of Viognier in front of *Ashes to Ashes*, being surprised by the arrival of an Ultravox retrospective box set you have no memory of buying or ever wanting is bound to play into Capitalism, Inc.'s hands. Previously, when you could only do shopping in real life, the only reasons you'd end up buying things you didn't want would be that the salesman had told you that gold lamé capri pants really help play down your nose or that you wanted *The Lovers' Guide* and you had to buy three medical textbooks as well so it looked like you just had a professional interest. Nowadays, we buy things we don't want all the time off the Internet. Not least because the Internet still doesn't feel like the real world, so it's almost as though subconsciously we don't think buying stuff off it counts. Theoretical money we've never seen, which was moved electronically into our accounts in the first place, is moved electronically to www.shityoudontneed.com, who send us a machine for turning eggshells into soap. With one-click ordering, we're barely involved in the transaction and the whole thing only begins to take on a tangible form when the all-too-tangible form of Big Dave from Chichester Debt Recovery and Thumping Services turns up at your door asking you how sold you are on keeping your gonads.

Health (Intellectual)

In not-that-far-bygone days, British people would maintain the roundedness of their characters with the pursuit of astonishing numbers of hobbies. That unassuming chap you sat next to on the bus every day with the side parting and the horn-rimmed specs was probably, at various points over his weekend, breeding rare birds, training for a triathlon in Corsica, undertaking an informal sub-aquatic archaeological survey at an abandoned Roman coal pit and ringing prostitutes and then putting the phone down in a panic when they answered. Now nobody does anything. They just spend all weekend updating their status on Facebook (apparently oblivious to the fact that whatever they write after 'Giles is . . .' it still basically reads as 'on Facebook again') and emailing each other videos of idiots getting their penis stuck in a whisk. Nobody creates their own stories any more; they just sit around looking at other people's while their brains dribble out of their nostrils.

Health (Physical)

You might think that the proliferation of the World Wide Web offered no real threat to the health of the nation, aside from the fact that, thanks to a combination of the Internet and that interminable bloody sale that seems to have been on at DFS since shortly before the Wars of the Roses, many of the British population have become so sedentary that they are now only really held together by surface tension. In fact, the Internet is one of the greatest challenges of this age to the NHS by dint of the fact that it's a hypochondriac's paradise. Where before if you felt a slight twinge in your belly you might have been inclined to imagine it to be a little wind brought on by the Brie-eating competition you had with Barry from Accounts at lunch, now you are able to Google your symptoms and within seven minutes end up with a number of diagnoses to suit every level of paranoia, ranging from stomach cancer to conjunctivitis to sleep apnoea to dropsy. Before you can say, 'Number of man-hours lost to sickness,' you're sitting in front of a GP who's rolling his eyes and asking if you've heard of Gaviscon. The truly dedicated cyber-chondriacs are themselves in danger because of their new-found access to how-to guides for emergency minor surgical procedures. Naturally, these are intended for professionals, but many of them are not password-protected against the large numbers of drama queens who have convinced themselves those pins and needles are deep-vein thrombosis and are within easy reach of an envelope knife and a stapler.

In many respects, though, the Internet was inevitable, being as it is the product of a dizzying rate of technological progress and humanity's insatiable desire for MODERN LABOUR-SAVING DEVICES.

MODERN LABOUR-SAVING DEVICES

My prevailing impression of the 1950s was formed on hearing Mr Leverton, who taught Russian at my school, describe it as having been 'dreary, like ten years of wet Sunday afternoons'. This from a man who was used to leading trips to Moscow in the 1970s and 1980s, and therefore ought to be credited with knowing a thing or two about dreary. His view is a fairly widely held one, but this notion of the buttoned-up, grey-as-old-skin SOCIETY of the time has always seemed to me at odds with the images handed down from popular culture to those of us who weren't there. As far as I understand it, there were essentially three types of female during the 1950s: borderline violent, sexually available school-girls who ran their teachers and the local bobby ragged; batty, ageing headmistresses who were really men in drag; and perma-waved wives with biologically unachievable pointy chests, who would stand in kitchens in deceptively undowdy A-line skirts, smiling and pointing at a top-loading washing machine. It is with this last group that we find the origins of our present culprit: Modern Labour-Saving Devices.

Modern Labour-Saving Devices were introduced in those very same 1950s. Before that time, no such things existed.[58] Back then, if you wished to, say, wash your clothes, you would be obliged either to go down to the nearest stream and bang them off a rock, working your fingers numb and singing songs featuring maidens combing their hair all in the month of May to keep your spirits up (country), or shuffle along to the pump in the market square to fetch some water and carry it home balanced on a yoke, looking for all the world like Stewart Hall was about to jump out and award you points (town). In the 1950s, all this changed when there was an explosion of Modern Labour-Saving Devices. In part this was because there was no longer a war on and engineers simply couldn't think of anything better to do, but mainly it was because they noticed that every time they made one, more perma-waved wives with biologically unachievable pointy chests would come and stand next to it, smiling. And if there's one thing engineers like, it's perma-waved wives with biologically unachievable pointy chests standing next to something they've invented, smiling. By the time the supply of these women had run out, to be replaced by the furious hippies of the 1960s, the genie was out of the bottle and there was nothing to

---

[58] Of course, there were earlier, more primitive labour-saving devices, namely the wheel and the slave trade, but both of those were controversial in their own way, except for the wheel.

be done – Modern Labour-Saving Devices were here to stay.

There's no doubt that Modern Labour-Saving Devices have their advantages. The invention of the answering machine, for example, has saved a lot of time that would previously have been spent picking up the phone and pretending to be an answering machine and then saying to the person on the other end the next time you met, 'Oh, yeah, they've got those now. An uncle of mine sent it from AMERICA. Oh, you'd like one? Ahm, unfortunately, I think they've run out. Limited edition or something.' The problem is that, much like the rules of THE HEALTH AND SAFETY EXECUTIVE, what is supposed to help us is actually causing humankind to de-evolve.

As noted elsewhere, one of the great contributing factors to the State of the World is humankind's bound-less capacity to take progress as an excuse to slack off. The more mental and physical tasks ticked off the list by Modern Labour-Saving Devices, the more the brain and body begin to atrophy. It is now possible to buy a fridge on the front of which is an LCD panel telling you what food it's out of.[59] The terrible implication of this is not that sufficient numbers of people thought

---

[59] Presumably, this is so you can tell the man from Ocado what to bring round for you so that you don't have to leave off watching *Heroes* to spend half an hour in the supermarket preventing your own death from starvation.

it was a good enough idea to get the thing made in the first place; it's that they were right – there is clearly a market for it. Have we really reached a point as a species where opening the fridge to have a quick check on whether the pesto's separated is seen as too much strain on elbow and brain? Yes. We have.

Our minds are turning to the kind of fatty clump you used to have to winkle out of the shower plughole with a straightened-out wire coat hanger before Mr Muscle came up with that excellent foamy stuff that does the job for you. Not only are we able to avoid having to learn new skills, but the store of knowledge we previously had seems to be depleting. The apotheosis of this is the pernicious effect on the nation's collective noggin felt following the rise of GPS systems. Every other car on the road now has one of those dashboard top boxes in which lives a well-spoken, bossy lady calmly giving instructions on the route ever so slightly too late. At first sight a boon, people have become so reliant on these devices that their ability to read a map, their sense of relative geography and ultimately their self-reliance have dribbled out of their ears and down that plughole Mr Muscle unblocked. Turning a GPS system off as you are driving, you feel a little like Luke Skywalker disconnecting his on-board computer as he makes his final sortie on the Death Star when what you should feel like is a person driving a Megane half a mile to Aldi.

Modern Labour-Saving Devices have contributed enormously to the inability (and sometimes simple refusal) of present-day humans to think for themselves. Even that wouldn't be so bad if it weren't for the fact that not thinking doesn't sit very happily with the modern default position of adamantly believing ourselves to be right about everything. That, after all, is how our government ended up following AMERICA into Iraq.

Recent research indicates that[60] if we continue to give over physical and mental ability to Modern Labour-Saving Devices at the current rate, within three generations evolution will have removed our fingers and replaced them with one enormous, RSI-proof, button-pushing spike.

Modern Labour-Saving Devices, of course, are a product of recent times. You could probably tell by the name if you just thought about it for a minute. So logically, there must be something about the modern era that has allowed for this proliferation of these mind-frittering doodads. There is indeed: the widespread extraction of OIL.

---

[60] For 'Recent research indicates that' please read 'Tell you what, I bet that'.

OIL

Now we turn to bubbling crude. Oil, that is. Black gold. Texas tea. It means different things to different people. To some, it is the very foundation of mankind's miraculous progress; to others, it is the single most unpleasant thing they've ever been forced to drink during an out-of-control team-building weekend. There are those for whom it is the lifeblood of commerce, while others are more inclined to view it as the thing that seems to be stopping them from flapping their wings. Whatever your view, however, Oil is at the heart of most of the problems that we all face today.[61]

Oil, as my great-uncle used to say, is the root of all evil.[62] It's one of those things that seemed like a good idea when we first came across it but which has subsequently proved to be more trouble than it's worth, like perms or the Olympics. It has certainly changed our lives in astonishing ways. If you had suggested to

[61] Except that weird thing on your leg. That's nothing to do with Oil, and you should really go and see someone about that.
[62] In fact, what he actually used to say was, 'Women are the root of all evil', but I think that was probably just a generational thing.

someone from the eighteenth century that a few generations down the line we'd all be careening about the skies in giant metal cheroots powered by liquefied mammoths, they would have told you to take your wig off once in a while to stop your head from overheating. However, for all that it has changed our lives for the better, it is this very same technological leap of apparent progress that has also given us Terminal 5 and that bit where the easyJet cabin crew try to impose their personality on the in-flight safety briefing.

As any student of modern history knows, however, there are much bigger problems with Oil than those posed by encountering frustrated cabaret turns in their day jobs. The key to these other problems is that Oil is the king of natural resources. The ownership of natural resources is very important,[63] and unfortunately they have been shared out around the world in a very uneven fashion, either by God or geology, depending on which set of men in sandals you think has a more plausible case. The good ones have been parcelled out to a few countries, like Japan (rice, which goes with everything) and Russia (gas – highly flammable and extremely dangerous but your only real option if you're after making a successful béchamel sauce), whereas other countries have come away with practically nothing, as in the case of Krygyztan (consonants – of limited use

[63] See RUSSIAN OLIGARCHS, p.103.

since proper nouns don't count in Scrabble). Inevitably, territorial disputes and aggression occur between the haves and the have-nots, as well as the haves and the have-but-want-to-have-mores. Really the whole of human history has been one big shit-fight over who has control of what. Lately the *casus belli* has tended to be Oil.[64] It is so desirable partly because it has transformed the areas in which it has been discovered: it saved Texas's reputation, lending credibility to the Texans' natural boastfulness, which had hitherto seemed a little misplaced when all they had to go on about was those big hats; it turned the Arabian Peninsula from a romantic, desolate land to a romantic, desolate land with some O'Neill's Irish pubs for the ex-pats; it turned Scotland into the country of wealthy, physically fit *bon viveurs* it is today. Who wouldn't want a piece of that? So it is that world peace can never be achieved.

Oil causes difficulties on a more specifically domestic front, too. These issues are usually linked to barrels of Oil, those poorly understood units of economic panic. No one knows how much they contain, what they ought to cost in a world that wasn't insane or what anyone's doing going round buying Oil in barrels in the first place; all they know is that when the price of them gets mentioned on the news, it's time to dig up

---

[64] Although water is beginning to run it close, being the cause of nastiness in areas as diverse as Sudan and the Evian region of France.

the lawn and rent some *Good Life* DVDs for tips on how to survive when the global economy breaks. Little is more likely to make the British people collectively take leave of reason than the suspicion that crude prices are about to precipitate a fuel crisis. Naturally enough, this is a self-fulfilling prophecy. Like a bunch of sheep – albeit highly organised sheep with access to buckets[65] – we thunder down to the all-night garage and queue up for hours, fill our buckets full of petrol, take them home, put them in the shed and declare, 'There! We're safe!' To which the correct reaction is, 'You're not safe – you've got buckets full of petrol in your shed.'

Perhaps, given its propensity to sow the seeds of discord, the most irritating aspect of Oil is its inherent can't-live-with-it-can't-live-without-it-ness. By means of war and economic gloom Oil has caused bloodshed, depression, unemployment, starvation, the temporary rescinding of moral codes and the destruction of homes and habitats. On the other hand, it goes to make DVDs of *Die Hard 3* and the handle of that grapefruit knife that's completely changed the way you eat breakfast, so swings and roundabouts, really.

The fiscal doom and the violence visited on us by Oil are only going to get worse as the supplies begin

---

[65] Farmers want to be on the lookout for that kind of development. It's precisely that sort of thing that would finally be the challenge to mankind's supremacy that we know must be coming some day.

to run out. If I remember correctly from watching *Tomorrow's World* in the early 1980s, they were due to run out a couple of years ago. Clearly, they haven't yet. Perhaps *Tomorrow's World* got it wrong, or perhaps since it stopped being on every Thursday, the number of people wasting Oil by using plastic to create ridiculous, unwieldy machines of negligible practical use just so they could get on the telly has delayed the inevitable. Whatever the reason, it will eventually go and the world will be plunged into the kind of dystopia rarely seen outside the bleak, post-apocalyptic *Play for Today*s that were on around the same time as those editions of *Tomorrow's World*, in which the last few remaining humans used to wander around desolate landscapes of skips filled with televisions, and rival quasi-tribal communities would wage long wars over a tin-opener.

In fairness, though, we have only continued to race through Oil like a soap star through vodka because we felt safe in the assumed knowledge that SCIENCE would find an alternative before anything got too serious. It hasn't. So maybe we should be blaming it instead.

SCIENCE

Hey, Science! Yeah, you – the kid in the corner with the impenetrable jargon and the Deep Purple T-shirt. We've got a bone to pick with you. In fact, we've got several bones. We've got, I would say, a modestly success-ful archaeology field trip's worth of bones to pick with you. Let me put it in language you can understand:

Hypothesis: that Science will make everything better.

Equipment: Science, life in general, the boundless human capacity for hopeless misunderstanding, conical flask (metaphorical).

Method: we mixed the life in general and the boundless human capacity for hopeless misunderstanding in a conical flask (metaphorical) and observed that the resulting mixture was largely inert. We added Science and observed that the solution went up like a Northern Rock shareholders meeting (circa 2007), shattering a nearby globe, causing blindness, panic and several people to hide in the fume cupboard.

Conclusion: 1) Science makes everything worse; 2) extended metaphors aren't as easy as they look.

The problem with you, Science, is that you are at best disappointing and at worst so terrifying on such a wide-spread scale that if you stick around much longer, Pampers could double their share price by branching out into grown-up sizes. Disappointing? I should say so. You swank about the place like Jimmy Big Pyjamas, making all sorts of claims that you never keep. Where's our stuff, Science? Where are all the cool things you promised us? At any point from about the 1950s onwards there's been a general assumption that thirty years on from wherever we happen to be there will be at least one and possibly all of the following: jet packs, flying cars, a monorail system 300 feet up in the air. So far, not a sausage. And certainly not an anti-gravity one. Where are they, Science? Where's my anti-gravity sausage? Was *Tomorrow's World* all a lie?

It's not just the fun stuff where you've let us down, either. You like to claim (usually in Nobel Prize accept-ance speeches or when a good way into a Stowells of Chelsea box at the *New Scientist* Christmas do) that your *raison d'être* or, as the French would say, your 'reason of to be' is to benefit the human race through the medium of progress brought about through experiment and discovery. But the truth is, Science, that from your very inception you have bought progress and misery with the same coin and in equal measure.[66] At the dawn of

[66] Note to readers: this is a metaphor. There isn't actually a shop where you can do that, so don't even bother Googling it.

mankind, there were only two known metals – gold and silver – and everyone was happy. But then along you trolled, Science, and developed bronze, which seemed tremendously useful for making pots and brooches at first, but which soon brought misery as children had to start learning about a whole new age in history lessons and the number of people winning medals that weren't gold doubled.

Oh, yes, it's all very good and fine going around the place, with your bowties and your periodic tables and your reassuringly academic-sounding middle-European accents, promising to make life easier to live, isn't it? But your preferred method of attempting this is by asking the kind of awkward questions that normal people – who simply want to sit on the sofa, eating Doritos and gawping at Amanda Lamb in another one of those remarkable tops – know are only to be found printed on the inside of a catering-sized can of worms and are therefore best left alone. Life was simple, Science, and you overcomplicated it.

You want chapter and verse? Well, *there's* an irony because over a period of millennia Judaeo-Christian clerics worked jolly hard at creating a plausible, simple vision of the way things are that everyone could understand which involved a nice old chap who made a series of concentric spheres in which he placed stars, angels, the Sun, the Earth, various other planets and a note saying that the clergy were in charge and should be given money, food and poontang. Then along came Galileo, who spoiled everything by pointing out that it wasn't true. The Catholic Church, concerned in part for the reputation of the nice old chap but with one eye on the supply of money, food and poontang, went off their institutional nut and used the powerful counterargument of threatening to kill him. This spat ushered in the terrifying age of uncertainty in which we now live by unhelpfully providing more than one point of view from which we have to choose. Thanks, Science.

Not only are you potentially costing us our souls, Science, but more important even than that, you're costing us actual proper money. This is because you've a bad habit of hanging around with some unsuitable types. You know your old mate Capitalism? Yes, you do – the one with the 'I heart China' T-shirt. Well, I've got news for you, Science – Capitalism is just using you to get to us. He's using you to terrify and bamboozle us into being impressed with what he has to offer in much the same manner and with much the same level of sophistication as a grandfather persuading a four-year-old that he's found some stairs behind the settee. Anyone sitting through all of the ad breaks in a single edition of *This Morning* is likely to have their brain assaulted (and insulted) by nonsensical, quasi-diagrammatic animations intended to explain yoghurt, poltroons wombling on about 'friendly bacteria' or omega-3 and A-list celebs telling you, 'Here comes the Science bit. Concentrate!'[67]

To cap it off, there's the sneaking[68] suspicion that you're going to kill us all. Sure, you've come up with some good ideas, but for every one of those there's an absolute kettleful of frog dross to balance it out. You gave us that button for indicating whether we're happy with the cleanliness in motorway services' toilets, but then again you gave us global warming. You gave us the motorised tie rack, but then again you gave us germ warfare. You gave us kidney dialysis machines, but then again you gave us the Death Star. Come on. Seriously. Don't you think you've got your priorities a little skewy?

One of the major problems with Science is that for all its claims to progress and building a better world and curing diseases and all that, it's not actually working for humanity at large, rather it's working for whichever terrifying pharmaceutical MULTINATIONAL or threatening foreign power or other organisation is paying the lab heating bills.

Of course, Science has found cures for AIDS and

---

[67] To which the correct response is, 'It's only a line going up on a graph, you dumb bint. Where were you when you were supposed to be in primary school?'

[68] I here mean 'sneaking' in the way that someone pushing marbles down a spiral staircase in a galvanised-steel wheelbarrow could be said to be 'sneaking'.

answers to global warming and a way of making the labels in clothes less scratchy. Why hasn't it let on to the rest of us? Because as with so many things, those answers are owned and suppressed by the group that paid for them, THE SECRET ALL-POWERFUL ORGANISATION THAT REALLY RUNS THE WORLD.

THE SECRET ALL-POWERFUL ORGANISATION THAT REALLY RUNS THE WORLD

Here's an experience we've all had: you know when you're on holiday in the Loire, right? You know when you're walking around a château on a guided tour and you wander off for a bit because you don't really speak French and that room behind the rope looks quite interesting, yeah? And you start trying to have a look at the back of the late-Victorian, eight-day gong-striking, four-glass mantle clock with mercury pendulum and visible escarpment above the fireplace, but you accidentally knock one of the candlesticks over with your elbow and a trapdoor opens at your feet and you find yourself sliding down the endless loops and curls of a metal chute? You know that, yeah? And you reach the end of the chute and drop into a leather armchair, and then you look around to see twenty or so identical armchairs ranged about a vast table carved of stone with ancient symbols from the six original civilisations etched into its rim, yeah? You know that?

And each of the other chairs is occupied by a figure in a robin's-egg-blue cassock, and then the one with the biggest hat, who's stroking an eagle perched on his starched white gauntlet, looks at you and says, 'At last we can begin.' Yeah? You know that, yeah? Well, did it ever occur to you to wonder who those people are? No? Well, you're going to feel foolish when I tell you. They, my friend, are the Secret All-Powerful Organisation That Really Runs the World. What do you mean, 'Which one?' *The* one. The one that all the conspiracy theorists believe in.

It makes sense now, doesn't it? All the clues were there: the globe in the corner with all those labels saying things like 'Bob's bit' and 'Property of Yuri – hands off!', the multi-ethnic security detail in black polo-neck jumpers with a hand-embroidered logo featuring an all-seeing eye above the insignia of the world's major religions; those lovely fruit baskets on the table . . .

So what exactly is this Organisation? you may be wondering. Over the years many different conspiracy theorists with many different axes to grind have made various groups the frontrunner. In good news for anti-Semites, the Jews have often been considered right up there as likely candidates. This unpleasant theory rather conveniently overlooks the fact that the Organisation goes paintballing on the third Saturday of every month and therefore cannot include any practising Jews among its members. Jews are, if anything, discriminated against by the Organisation in this respect. The Masons, then, it must be the Masons, you say. Again, no. Although it is traditional to imagine the Masons sitting in their Grand Lodges divvying up the business world, apportioning the hair-dressing concessions for east Leicestershire to this member and the Aberdeenshire pond-lining dollar to that member, in practice this sort of thing very rarely happens. Masons have little time left over after sitting around making up archaic, proto-mythic nonsense on which to base their silly boys' club to do any real harm. So, then, you ask again, what exactly is this Secret All-Powerful Organisation That Really Runs the World?

Well, its official name is the Secret All-Powerful Organisation That Really Runs the World. At least, that's what it's lodged as at Companies House. They were originally going to try and think up some sort of snappy brand-name-type moniker to make themselves seem more relevant to the Kids, but every time they came up with one, this guy in the marketing department would tell them that it meant something rude in one language or another.

The Organisation itself has quite a complex structure, owing in large part to the tremendously knotty logistics involved in secretly running the world.[69] Most importantly for us, though, is the Council of Twenty-One, which makes up the top layer of management and who are to all intents and purposes the ones doing the world-running. These figures are surprisingly diverse. Naturally, there are one or two prime ministers and presidents in there, along with notable business leaders. Perhaps more unexpectedly, there's a guy who runs a corner shop in Bridlington. He's there because when the Organisation started out and hadn't yet excavated their own subterranean lair, they used to meet in his stockroom every Wednesday afternoon and they felt it seemed a bit unfair not to include him. This is a good example of how the Organisation hadn't really got the hang of ruthlessness in the early days. Two others also numbered amongst the Twenty-One are a geography teacher – whose job it is to clear up territorial issues such as 'In which administrative territory does Berwick currently fall?' and 'Why is Guyana?' – plus Patti Boulaye, not for her role as a Conservative Party activist, but because it was part of the prize awarded her for being the only contestant ever to achieve the maximum score of 120 points on *New Faces*. Also, someone from Tesco.

---

[69] This has always been one of the drawbacks of successful megalomania. Very few would-be demagogues ever take into account the sheer amount of admin involved should they achieve their dreams of subjugating people to their will. This inability to think things through in a wider context is one of the principal downsides of monomania, along with not being very good at small talk.

The Secret All-Powerful Organisation That Really Runs the World can, of course, be held directly or indirectly to blame for absolutely everything. Think of the single thing that annoys you most about modern life. Be it dogs in handbags, the silly bitches holding the dogs in the handbags, the press pack who hound the silly bitches with the dogs in the handbags or even something completely different, like famine or rudeness, the Organisation is to blame. The banks, the POLITICIANS, the media, the corporations, not a single one of them escapes the hand of the Organisation. Our entire lives, even without us knowing it, are directed by and to the benefit of its members. Ultimately, through their manipulation of the institutions of our world, there is nothing for which the Secret All-Powerful Organisation That Really Runs the World cannot be held to blame.

Which would be perfect for our purposes, except that it doesn't exist. Oh. Shame.

That isn't to say that there isn't an all-powerful organisation made up of mysterious and colourful members with a penchant for secrecy and a staggering amount of global influence; it's just that they're called RUSSIAN OLIGARCHS.

RUSSIAN OLIGARCHS

Ingratitude is a terrible thing. This is why my wife and I have created a database on our computer detailing all the unpleasant gifts we have ever been sent and which of the people who claim to know us had the lapse of taste responsible for our ending up with the revolting thing. Next, through a canny piece of software called iSore, we are able to cross-reference this database with our diary, allowing our computer to warn us of the imminent arrival of guests and which foul doodad they would be offended not to see on our mantelpiece. Then, using the ten-digit reference the iSore alert has given us, we are able to go down to our purpose-built storage facility[70] and extract the Jesus made of almond shells or the ceramic vagina or whatever. It takes a tremendous amount of effort, but we do at least manage never to appear ungrateful.

This, I think, is my main problem with Russian Oligarchs. It's the bare-arsed ingratitude that really

[70] You know that bit at the end of *Raiders of the Lost Ark* when the guy wheels the ark in a wooden crate down into a massive underground hangar of practically identical wooden crates? That's the sort of thing.

sticks in my craw. We in the West spent generations having our very best people try to promote capitalism to the Soviets – Richard Nixon, George Smiley . . . there must have been others – and now that they've finally got it, these Russian Oligarchs have had what I can only describe as the ruddy nerve[71] to be better at it than us.

Russia was once a simple place, easy to deal with – a cold and forbidding land whose people passed their days queuing for hours in the snow to buy vodka and big hats and committing suicide over doomed love affairs. Its army was threateningly large and well armed, but mainly used for ceremonial marching and providing employment for men who were unable to bend their legs at the knee, if the May Day parades in Red Square are anything to judge by.[72] The whole caboodle was overseen by sour-faced Bolshevik generals played by Steven Berkoff who considered the Kremlinites recidivist pansies and were forever trying to hijack the military to start a war with the West. We didn't like them;[73] they didn't like us.[74] It was easy.

[71] 'Bally cheek' might have worked here as well.

[72] It says much for the Soviets' media management that in the footage of the May Day parades that was released to the West, we only ever got to see the quite-threatening floats that had things like great big missiles on them, while the other, more fun floats that had classes of schoolchildren on them singing medleys from *Annie* were edited out.

[73] Except the Beatles.

[74] Except the Beatles.

Nowadays, the situation is more complicated. Russia may still be a land of vodka, hats and suicides,[75] but it also seems to have become what Chicago in the 1920s might have been like if it had been styled by Hermès and Louis Vuitton. The place is all emaciated, heavily made-up prozzies and burly chaps in leather jackets running illegal caviar-faking rackets. This all started to happen around the time that the Russians changed their style of national leader from the time-honoured 'stony-faced sociopath' kind to the rather newer kind who used to get drunk and stand on tanks, waving, looking for all the world like someone had stuck one end of a foot pump up their fundament and was giving it all they were worth.

Emerging from this drinking-game-based political landscape came the Russian Oligarchs – a group of men who'd cannily seized the opportunity in the dying days of communism to see if the heads of Russia's various state OIL and gas concerns would swap them for a pair of Levi 501s. Came the answer, 'Make it stonewashed and you've got a deal.'

The long-term effect of this on the State of the World has been twofold. Firstly, the Russian Oligarchs have annoyed all the other capitalists by making them look rubbish. To be fair, Bill Gates's thirty years spent climbing

---

[75] Incidentally, 'Russia – Land of Vodka, Hats and Suicides' was only narrowly rejected by the Russian Tourist Federation as the country's official advertising slogan.

to the top of the Forbes 400 by becoming the architect of the modern age looks like simple time-wasting next to the men who spent about seventeen minutes securing half a hemisphere's natural reserves for their own profit. Secondly, and more importantly, it has placed us directly at the mercy of powerful Russians for the first time since Gorbachev had the bedside nuclear button in the Kremlin disconnected in case he accidentally hit it while he was feeling around for his reading specs.

Russian Oligarchs now control many of the pipelines into the West that are used not only for transporting spies on automated luges, but for supplying gas. This means that our Once-Great Nation can effectively be shut down by a minor official made good who's cross that the Monopolies and Mergers Commission won't let him buy any more football clubs. This in turn means that we have to be nice to these people, and being nice to foreigners is simply not what Britain is all about (cf. Immigration, our casually racist attitude towards other European nationalities, the entire history of THE BRITISH EMPIRE . . .).

Russian Oligarchs are a direct attack on the confidence of the people who keep our markets afloat, the cause of jitters about energy sources – and therefore to blame for the government's decision to condemn us all to nuclear power for decades to come – and, to top it all, compelling us to behave entirely contrary to our national character.

However, the Russian Oligarchs' power is waning. They're a bit 1990s, truth be told. This leaves room for someone else to take their threatening place. The new threat from the East coming to fill the vacuum and then sell it back to us is CHINA.

CHINA

China, or as you may be more familiar with it, Made in China, or to give it its full title, the People's Republic of Made in China, represents the greatest threat today to the way we live. As threats go, it's a pretty good one; in exactly the same way as the Middle East, it fulfils all the modern criteria for a looming shadow over our very existence:

1. It's a long way away.

2. Very few of us understand what they are saying over there.

3. People who've visited it say that the food isn't like the stuff they serve in their restaurants over here and we don't know what the hell that's all about.

4. We only realised about two years ago that they have a lot of technology and seem to be very good at it.

5. It's hard to accept 4., because until we noticed it, we imagined that life there was basically like a G. A. Henty novel – all spies and thieves and secret societies and escaping from palaces in rolled-up carpets.

Essentially, what we know about China is that we don't know a lot but that the people who do know a lot (Paxman, Kaplinsky, all the greats) seem to be talking about it as the place all our jobs and money are about to go. There are, as we understand things, two basic causes of the current recession.[76] The first is the development of sub-prime mortgages – the lately discredited practice among American mortgage brokers of giving loans for the purchase of duplexes on Central Park West to people who do the weekday batter-mixing shift at KFC. The second is China. Since any slide towards recession is exacerbated by fear of the unknown, China is the more significant of these two. We thought we knew about China, but it turns out we don't – it's not all waving porcelain cats and brutal repression over there after all – and everything we learn about the place puts further into context how little we actually do know and thus serves to hammer another nail into the coffin of the Happy, Happy Boom Years.

[76] If at the point in the future during which you are reading this book there is no recession, then please replace it on the bookshelf until there is. Thank you for your cooperation in this matter.

First of all, there is the business of China's cities. For centuries there were only two Chinese cities, Peking and Shanghai.[77] A little while ago, those two became three when they were joined by Beijing. Some time later, it turned out that someone had translated the press release wrong and that Beijing and Peking were in fact the same. This brought China back to having only two cities again, which if anything looked more like economic decline. You can't just lose a third of your major cities like that and expect people to consider you an economic contender. Is it any wonder that this whole thing has taken us by surprise? At any rate, there are now many more than two Chinese cities. We've never heard of any of them before; they're all bigger than Mexico and Chad put together, and they all suffer from terrible smog. We only know this much because the Sunday supplements run features on one or other of them every three weeks, usually accompanied by a panoramic view of the city in question in a smog-red sunset with the silhouette of a bicycling Chinese worker wearing a face mask in the foreground. How can there be so many massive metropolises of which we had been hitherto unaware? It's hard to avoid the obvious – and very threatening – conclusion that the Chinese have the technology and the manpower to build a new one every three weeks.

[77] Thinking about it, there might have been Kowloon, but on the other hand that also might have been a type of boat.

Then there is the fact that, thanks to the famous 'one-child' policy, it turns out China has the fastest-ageing population in the world. The implications here are twofold. Firstly, those herbal anti-ageing remedies your friend Marita gets from that weird little shop in Chinatown probably aren't up to much, and she's not going to be happy about that because she's been on them for months and for something that smells like someone found a sock in a drain, they're pretty expensive. Secondly, China is exponentially increasing the stock of one of its greatest natural resources: Wise Old Men. For many years, during the great boom in China's population, life was difficult for Wise Old Men. Overcrowding meant that often as many as three Wise Old Men had to share the same mountaintop cave, which led to confusion and jealousy when pilgrims turned up looking for guidance from one of them in particular.[78] However, with the increased urbanisation discussed earlier, Wise Old Men now have no need to live in mountaintop caves at all, as there is plenty of accommodation for everyone, and they have come into the cities to live. This, along with their burgeoning numbers, means that those running the already fairly robust Chinese economy practically have Wise Old Men on tap to make sure they're pointing in the right

---

[78] The need for more mountains in which to house Wise Old Men was one of the principal factors behind the Chinese invasion of Tibet.

direction. And that's something that the West simply can't compete with.

The Chinese economic miracle might have been good for China, but one of the immediate and more unwelcome consequences has been the effect on global warming. This has been in some measure due to the amount of crap that floats out of big chimneys when of necessity half your manufacturing base is given over to producing those little peanut-shaped polystyrene things that you use for packing everything that the other half of your manufacturing base makes. Added to this is the fact that China's PR department is keenly aware that the smog is what keeps getting it in the Sunday supplements. China's attitude to global warming means that its businesses and the West's businesses are not playing on a level turf. Until recently, China was able to do pretty much what it liked as far as the environment was concerned.[79] Businesses in the West, on the other hand, were subject to highly restrictive regulations forcing them at least to pay lip service to the idea of environmentalism, a practice costing valuable time that could otherwise have been spent concocting more spurious arguments against the minimum wage. Now that China has decided for diplomatic reasons to start paying such lip service itself, regulations have tightened for Western businesses, so that they

[79] Which is why all the pandas started disappearing – they were being put to work shovelling anthracite in coal-burning power stations.

now have to indulge in more green-friendly practices, such as putting a thing at the bottom of their emails asking the recipient if they really need to print it out. Naturally enough, the Chinese have Western economies at their mercy.

Frankly, though, China shouldn't have been able to get so far with their own economic domination of the world when the kind of human-rights abuses they visit on the people within their borders would meet a furious regime of sanctions if they were perpetrated by less awkwardly successful countries. The blame for that lies, as you might imagine, very much with THE UNITED NATIONS.

THE UNITED NATIONS

Conventional wisdom[80] among the British has it that Belgium is a boring little country with not a lot to interest those not either born there or with a poorly monitored EU expense account.[81] So entrenched is this notion that tourists from the UK largely avoid it in spite of the fact that it is the most obviously appropriate place for them to take their holidays, being as it is the producer *par excellence* of the four Great British loves: beer, chips, chocolate and unjustified casual racism towards the French. Behind the idea lies the assumption that Belgians would love to be less boring but simply don't have the get-up-and-go. *Au contraire.* Belgium has spent a long time developing unexcitement to an exacting and precise standard. So cutting edge is that country's deliberate

---

[80] Which is another way of saying, 'What people who can't be bothered doing a bit of research think . . .' or, 'Wikipedia says . . .'

[81] An idea made all the more amusing by the fact that Belgium has two national identities to choose from and still can't muster anything about itself that might warrant so much as a 'Did You Know?' fact on a sugar packet.

unremarkableness that it even decided to indulge in a months-long experiment to see whether having absolutely no government at all would make matters even more sedate, since politics was getting a bit too colourful and threatening to raise the collective national heart rate above the level of a 'lub' one week and a 'dub' the next.

What, you might wonder, lies behind this odd decision to attract as little attention as possible? It is so very far from the modus operandi of most modern nations, which simply clamour to be heard: AMERICA by developing and then aggressively marketing **DEMOCRACY!** (an ineffective potato-print version of the more famous DEMOCRACY, painted in primary colours and inserted into justifications for war); CHINA by whipping an economy out of nowhere in the greatest act of national conjuring since Germany broke out the Black Forest gateaux[82] while Britain was still working out how to fry powdered eggs; North Korea by behaving like a cross between the East Germany of John le Carré novels and Greta Garbo.

Belgium's deliberate – and highly successful – attempt to eschew excitement is the direct result of having been chosen as the venue for the First World

[82] So many Black Forest gateaux, in fact, that there was a glut which lasted well into the 1970s. The backlog was only cleared by the clandestine German strategy of inventing the Berni Inn.

War[83] and seeing many of its towns razed to the ground and citizens slaughtered as a result of what can only be described as quite remarkable on-field violence. Faced with the aftermath of a war so devastating that it made a perfectly good country stop behaving like a country at all, the international community perhaps unsurprisingly decided that it ought at the very least to get together for tea and cakes once in a while and see if it couldn't just talk its problems out over a lapsang souchong instead of sending whole generations to their death. So it was that the League of Nations was born. The success of the League of Nations can be measured by the fact that the word 'first' appears before the words 'world' and 'war' in the phrase 'the First World War'. After the Second World War,[84] the League countries decided to get back together again and give it one more go, which, as any soap-opera fan will tell you, is a common delusion doomed to inevitable failure. Thus was formed the United Nations, a body that in terms

[83] Conventional wisdom (see footnote 80) among the British has it that the First World War was played between Great Britain and Germany, which might make the choice of Belgium as the venue somewhat puzzling, but it is worth noting that events of the magnitude of the First World War or the UEFA Cup final are usually played on neutral soil so that neither side has a home advantage.

[84] Which, unlike the First World War, was a draw after the standard period of four years' fighting (two years each way) and so went into extra time.

of being to blame for the State of the World can best be classed as 'Very'.

The United Nations' avowed intent is to promote worldwide peace. The main method it has employed in pursuit of this goal thus far has been the construction of a large building in New York in which you can, by observation, learn how to tut exasperatedly in all the languages of the globe. Occasionally, there may seem to be some sort of energised activity taking place within its walls, but it usually turns out to be no more than another lively speech from Hugo Chávez, hopping up and down in one of his crazy Venezuelan sweaters.[85] To no one's real surprise, the whole keeping-the-peace thing hasn't really worked.

The great problem with the UN is that it has written a pretty substantial cheque that it has absolutely no hope whatsoever of cashing. It has no standing armed forces, preferring instead to put its faith in the power and persuasiveness of words. In fairness, words can often be very powerful and persuasive, but that is only generally the case when those words are 'We have standing armed forces.' Consequently, the UN is reliant on its members volunteering to put their troops at its disposal. Naturally

[85] In front of that wall of odd green marble that gives every major speech made in the UN the look of someone standing in front of the mirror in an upmarket men's room, drunkenly rehearsing what they'd really like to say to their shit of a boss if they could ever pluck up the courage.

enough, many refuse or send fewer troops than they might as they are reluctant to spare them from their other duties such as making films (AMERICA), using fancy dress to boost the economy through tourism (Britain) or putting the finishing touches to the Maginot Line (France). This reluctance to commit resources stems in part from a wish to avoid expense but is mainly a result of the fact that the UN sticks soldiers in white uniforms. These are an absolute bugger to keep clean and have to be washed separately from the rest, causing a great deal of extra work. Not to mention being bad for the environment.[86] Occasionally, the UN does manage to cobble together a platoon or two to go driving round some political hotspot in tanks painted a subtle shade of target-practice white, but even then its basic peace-keeping tactic is the military equivalent of a man standing in a pub car park at eleven thirty on a Friday night saying, 'Hey, hey, hey, come on now, we've all had a few drinks,' while two big lads have it out on the bonnet of his Corolla.

It's not really fair to see the United Nations as emasculated, since its whole problem is that it was never really masculated in the first place, but there's no doubt

[86] Not enough attention is paid to green issues in the planning and execution of warfare. For example, under the terms of the Geneva Protocol, armies are forbidden to use biological weapons, and yet these work at much lower temperatures than non-biological weapons and are thus better for the environment as a whole.

that the overall feeling that the UN is one part good intentions to two parts piss and vinegar has somewhat stymied its ability to prevent anything much, from unprecedented internecine slaughter on a catastrophic scale in the Sudan to delegates failing to stack their used lunch trays on the trolleys provided in the canteen. It is the UN's complete failure to be any good at the job it set itself that allowed the self-styled Coalition of the Willing to mount the most misguided military operation since the last time a Roman tribune thought he'd have a crack at Asterix's village. And here is where the UN really starts to be to blame as far as this country is concerned.

The Iraq War has, if we've decided that we're going to spend today putting things mildly, caused a bit of resentment here or there. Now, if anyone should be used to being on the wrong end of a bit of resentment, it's Britain – a country that spent most of the eighteenth and nineteenth centuries pursuing a proactive foreign policy that consisted of sailing about the place nicking other people's natural resources and telling them that it was for their own good. However, the perpetratees of the perpetrations that we were perpetrating didn't choose to express their displeasure by exploding themselves in the middle of a thoroughfare busy with orange-sellers and coach-and-fours and princesses and plague victims and whatever else it was they had in the olden days.

These days, though, the people feeling the resentment have developed much more of a pro-exploding-themselves agenda and we have ended up with a country in which paranoia, racial tension and insularity among the populace at large are at the kind of levels that Oswald Moseley could only have dreamed of, and he had some pretty whacked-out dreams. (There was that one with the three Cinderellas asking him what sort of peanuts he'd like with his mint julep. And the one where he couldn't smell lavender. And that other one where the Jews were to blame for everything.)

But then a United Nations is only as good as the nations it's claiming to unite. If, say, one of them were to decide that it had had enough of listening to Security Council resolutions and was more inclined to see what would happen if you were to add the word 'gunboat' to the word 'diplomacy' to make 'gunboat diplomacy' and then get rid of the word 'diplomacy' to leave you with 'gunboat', there might be problems. Step forward, AMERICA.

AMERICA

I'll tell you what America's like: it's like a great big, overenthusiastic St Bernard's. A great big, overenthusiastic St Bernard's that can't help chasing squirrels. A great big, overenthusiastic St Bernard's that can't help chasing squirrels through a centuries-old Murano glass emporium, leaving the owners with a colossal mess to clean up and no chance of claiming on anyone else's insurance.

No, in fact it's like an uptight head girl. An uptight head girl with an acid tongue who holds court every lunchtime, keeping the cool kids in place around her with a stream of zingers and verbal bitch-slaps, until one of them answers back and she goes absolutely apeshit, screaming round the prefects' common room with her bra out.

Actually, I know what America's like: it's like the child you have that seems a little slow at first but that you're sure is just developing a bit more sedately than all the other children but that, by the time it reaches its teenage years, is so plainly dumb that as much as you love it, you can't help hoping that your wife was having an affair around the time of its conception.

Wait, no, I know. It's like the midsummer fair that pitches up on the common – bright, glitzy, fun, appealing, but run by people you wouldn't want to cross, and the relentless, threatening, thudding noise that emanates from it stops you from sleeping properly at night.

Or maybe it's more like a night with a stranger spent dangling your legs from a Venetian pontoon and talking and drinking amaretto until the sun comes up over St Mark's and you stagger back to her hotel and the sex is amazing, but two days later it turns out you picked up cholera from putting your feet in the canal.

Or maybe it's a vicar who's big on muscular Christianity and bench-pressing boxes of King James versions in front of the altar to demonstrate theological points but is always found at the summer fayre, moments after winning the Guess the Weight of the Cake competition that he fixed, crouching in the scout-hut kitchenette with chocolate all down his cassock and the head of a marzipan disciple sticking out of his mouth.

Or maybe it's like a cocky sushi chef who's only completed the first three years of Raw Fish School and hasn't covered the tough stuff yet but has seen enough people carving up a deadly blowfish to think he can give it a go and who, after accidentally poisoning all of the dinner-party guests his girlfriend begged him not to try stuff out on, takes the leftovers next door and asks if they'd like them.

No, I'll tell you what America's like: it's like the cup of coffee that they give you at your annual appraisal that the boss's secretary accidentally put salt in instead of sugar but that you don't draw attention to at first and consequently have to keep drinking so that your boss doesn't think you're some kind of idiot and give half your accounts to that moron Kevin who's joined the same golf club as him so that he can 'bump into' him in the clubhouse and pretend to have got round the course with a much worse stroke count.

Although, actually, no, it's like a really promising-sounding picnic organised by someone who's well known for organising really good picnics, where they've excelled themselves this time by flying everybody out to a private island off Trinidad populated entirely by the kind of nubile, booty-hipped concubines who wear those coconut bikinis that used to be really popular in 1950s cartoons, and hiring Dickie Bird to umpire the beach cricket afterwards, but when you get there, it turns out that everybody's brought the same kind of sandwiches.

Hang on, no, America's more like that thing when you try to fizz up a milkshake in a Soda-Stream and it seems like you're going to get something that's strawberry-flavoured and tingly and creamy but in the end it just goes all over the worktop and clogs up the nozzle on the machine and your dad comes in just at the wrong moment and goes off his cake with fury and you get sent to your room and told you can't go shopping to town with your mate Andy tomorrow like you'd planned, which means that there's no chance of getting hold of the new 'Final Countdown' 12-inch by Europe before your arch-nemesis Stephen 'Dukey' Robertson does and you know that means he'll spend the next week taunting you about it in school in front of Alice Claybury and she'll giggle and you'll start having to avoid the classroom at breaktime because of the embarrassment and it'll put your plan to pluck up the courage to ask her if she wants to go for a walk in the park back by another two years again.

No, tell you what: America's like one of those beautifully preserved, Ancient Grecian marble statues that are proportioned so exquisitely that you remark upon it to your wife and then she takes it the wrong way and points out that the statue hasn't had to squeeze out three kids (which were quite frankly unnaturally heifer-sized and they certainly don't get that from her side of the family, thank you very much) and you try to backtrack and explain that you were just appreciating the art and she says in a pointed tone that she's seen you appreciating art before and what about that little number at the Christmas party who seemed to be spending quite a long time next to the punch bowl with you and you have to tell her not to be so ridiculous and then she squeals, 'Ridiculous, am I?' and you ask her not to make a scene in the art gallery and she says that she can think of few better places and this is probably what Tracey Emin would do and you say that she's not Tracey Emin she's a reasonable person and your wife says that she thinks Tracey Emin is an entirely reasonable person who is simply characterised as otherwise by a media whose high-art section is populated by bitter old queens who wouldn't know talent if it came up and propositioned them on Clapham Common and you say you're going to wait in the car and she shouts an expletive after you and you have to apologise to the gallery attendant under your breath as you leave but you're pretty sure your wife's heard you and it's only going to make matters worse once you get home.

Or is it like a drunk playing the spoons in an orchestra? Or two men called Terence arguing over which one is more Terencey? Or a top CEO gluing pencil shavings to his face so he can sneak into a lepers' conference? Or a meat-smuggler hiding 4 tons of regular-width salami in a bamboo scaffold?

Well, anyway, you know what America's like. It doesn't matter in truth – we can't really blame America when we created it in the first place. If anything, America itself can be blamed on THE BRITISH EMPIRE.

THE BRITISH EMPIRE

The British Empire. A period in history beloved of old people and the kind of halfwits who aren't sure whether *Sharpe* is a documentary or not. It is for many the benchmark by which all subsequent periods in British history have been measured and found wanting. It was, or passed for in their minds, a golden age in which for one brief, heat-shimmering moment the natural order intended by God asserted itself and we as a nation were able to storm about the place in erotically tight scarlet outfits, thieving monuments and entering into frottery with native women.[87] However, as much as these people might be inclined to paint the British Empire as nothing worse than an extended business trip that got a little out of hand, it is more than possible to see in it the source of much that is wrong with the State of Things today.

---

[87] I suspect that a good deal of the contemporaneous enthusiasm for imperial conquest had its roots in the fact that English boys were able to get off with girls they only couldn't talk to properly because of the language barrier, as opposed to because of the more usual crushing fear of women imparted by having been brought up in England.

The Economy

Britain treated its imperial period in much the same way that an unemployed housewife from a sink estate treats a two-minute trolley dash round a Sainsbury's Savacentre. For hundreds of years we were able to take home good things to eat and wear at very reasonable prices thanks to our cast-iron negotiating technique of killing the people who'd owned them in the first place. Unfortunately, this gave us a taste for good things: spices, coffee, silk, tea, baklava, dupiazas, Bombay mix and anything that tastes of, well, actual food. Once we'd entirely voluntarily and amicably withdrawn from all the countries that we were helping with infrastructure out of the goodness of our hearts, we simply couldn't go back to eating whatever it was we were eating before; we still craved the produce of the former Greater Great Britain. Now, of course, they have us over a barrel. Maybe even one of the same barrels from that barrel factory we set up with slave labour back in the old days. I bet they're enjoying that irony. They can ask us pretty much what they want for their produce and we have to pay it. That's why you see so many rich Africans. Well, you do if you've seen *Coming to America* as often as I have.

Relations (International)

The thing about spending centuries lording it over the rest of the world with the kind of venality and arrogance with which the British conducted themselves is that when you finally get knocked off your perch, you're going to spend quite a long time having to eat poo. My generation of what tabloid journalists and Americans refer to as 'Brits' have the feeling of awkwardness towards the former colonies pretty much ingrained. Our attitude towards the British Empire is essentially 'I'm terribly sorry but we seem to have invaded your entire country. We've stayed two hundred years and raped all your natural resources – what an appalling *faux pas*. Oh, dear me. Well, if we could just borrow a cup of sugar, we'll be off. Here, have railways and DEMOCRACY by way of a trade-off; I'm afraid we've lost the instructions. Good luck.'

Now no one is really going to give Britain what it wants in international negotiations, because it's behaved so badly. You can see it on the news footage of the Commonwealth[88] Heads of Government Meeting

---

[88] As the ex-British Empire is now called. This change of title is an excellent example of geo-political face-saving. It was an empire; now it's not an empire. Britain looks a bit sad, so all the former colonies reluctantly agree to let it call them the Commonwealth. This is much like a former girlfriend telling you that you'll always have a special place in her heart to stop you from sitting outside her house playing 'The First Cut Is the Deepest' over and over again on the stereo of your Yaris.

– the other leaders looking at each other and raising their eyebrows slightly as Britain enters the room, as though to say, 'The *nerve* of that one, turning up after what she's done.' 'Leave it, Gladys. Don't bring yourself down to her level.'

In any case, it's not that easy to recommend your worldview to everybody else when, thanks to one or two historical points, you've had to vacate the moral high ground in favour of the kind of people whose supporters spend most of the daylight hours ululating in front of foreign news crews while waving Kalashnikovs and burning the flags of whomever it was this time who foolishly pointed out that impaling women for reading *Bella* might be a bit last century. This is one of the reasons that Britain has been forced to leave the role of global policeman to AMERICA[89] – they, after all, are only an imperial power in the currently fashionable (and therefore acceptable) capitalist sense, whereas we were an imperial power in the slightly less-favoured what-an-interesting-bit-of-marble-Have-it-packed-and-sent-to-Bloomsbury sense.

Relations (Domestic)

You know how when you go on holiday and you meet another couple (Keith and Barbara – he's something

---

[89] A role that they've taken to with the same gusto that domestic American policemen took to Rodney King.

big in the world of stamp glue, and she organises charity gymkhanas; nice enough people but a bit dull), you always say to them at the end of the week, 'Listen, if you're ever around Littlehampton, you *must* drop by,' but if they ever showed up, you'd be absolutely mortified? (A ring at the doorbell one day: 'Darling! You'll never guess! It's what's-his-name and Barbara. How embarrassing. Put the kettle on.') Well, much the same happened in the dying days of the British Empire. When Britain finally got out of all the countries it had been occupying, it said to the inhabitants, 'Listen, if you're ever around Britain, you *must* drop by.' Then, when they started accepting the invitation in the 1950s, Britain was indeed mortified. (A ring at the doorbell: 'Darling! You'll never guess! It's what's-his-name and Africa. How embarrassing. Put the giant kettle on.') This rather stiff, reluctantly semi-accommodating attitude did not bode well for what has been a pretty rollercoaster half-century of race relations in this country, but perhaps it was inevitable, given how embarrassing it is to address one's own personal wrong-doings with the actual wrongdoees. Remember how you cringed as a child when your dad hauled you round to Mr and Mrs Lampone's to apologise for wrapping their dog in cling film? Well, imagine Britain having to go round apologising to the owners of about a quarter of the dogs on the planet. It's more or less like that. And remember how unconvinced Mr and Mrs

Lampone found your forced *mea culpa*? Well, it's more or less like that, too. I mean, not in any real or helpful sense, but I don't think that weakens the point.

It is precisely this kind of ongoing, unpleasant social awkwardness that leads a British population simply incapable of coping with such things for more than five minutes, let alone the better part of sixty years, to start blaming the people making it embarrassed in the first place, IMMIGRANTS.

IMMIGRANTS

I think we all know who's really to blame for the state of this country, don't we? I think we can all guess who I mean, can't we? Well, we should be able to – it's written at the top of this page; I don't know how I can make it any clearer. To be honest, if you weren't able to guess who I meant, then perhaps I should be spending my time blaming something else instead, like the education system. Anyway, now we've all gone back and read the top of the page properly, we definitely know who I mean, don't we?

Immigrants.

That's right, Immigrants. Bunch of blood-sucking, sponging, freeloading, benefit smash-and-grab merchants, that's all they are. There. I've said it. It's not fashionable, but I've said it[90]. Still, if we're going to avoid the bleatings of namby-pamby lefties mewling about why you shouldn't generalise, we're going to have to be scrupulously fair in our definition, so allow me to qualify my assertion. Naturally enough, I don't

[90] Actually, it *is* fashionable, but 'It is fashionable, but I've said it' isn't a phrase.

mean to include every single immigrant group who has ever come to this country. For example, the Vikings were OK. Sure, they used to come on a bit heavy with the old raping and pillaging shtick, but what you have to remember is that attitudes were different in those days and most non-victims at least were able to shrug it off as high spirits. On the plus side, the Vikings contributed Jorvik and flat-pack furniture, along with those helmets with horns which you often see being worn by touring amateur rugby clubs in the pub of an evening, as they channel their repressed homosexuality into a series of tuneless, lewd ballads about the travel arrangements of small numbers of Scottish virgins.

The Normans, they were fine, too. You might not have liked them at the time, but they won that battle fair and square, and any country that's serious about war has got to respect that. Plus, they were basically Vikings with classier furniture and French O level, so you knew where you were with them.

Then of course the Jews started coming here at the invitation of William the Conqueror to help kick-start commerce, finance and trade, which was excellent news all round as inflation had hit the bartering system very badly at that point and a lot of people were putting their backs out carrying horses around with them on the off-chance they decided to nip off for a pint after tilling the fields. While we're on financiers, the Lombards who started migrating to England in the thirteenth century were pretty cool, too, even if they did bring that annoying blue cartoon phone that keeps popping up asking if you want a low-cost loan when you're trying to watch the telly with your family.

Around about the same time, of course, there were the Weavers from the Low Countries, who quite frankly couldn't have come over with their skills and technology a moment too soon, since the whole population up to that point would waste astonishing numbers of man-hours wrapping twine round themselves to form makeshift smocks before leaving their hut every morning. And then once the Weavers had sorted people out with proper clothes, it was nothing short of a godsend that the gypsies turned up a couple of hundred years later to put an end to two centuries of clothes blowing off washing lines.

It almost goes without saying that the contribution of the Huguenots, who began arriving in the sixteenth century, was vital to Great British culture, since it was the skill in lacework that they brought with them as they fled across the Channel that allowed for the invention of the doily, which would later become perhaps the single most significant decorative artefact of the imperial era and would more or less come to define the Victorian and Edwardian periods. So obviously, I'm not including them either.

Or the African immigrants of the eighteenth and

nineteenth centuries, really, since they can only properly be termed Immigrants if you decide that being forcibly taken from your home and asked politely but firmly to leave the ship somewhere a lot colder can be termed immigration. Still, we've a lot to thank those guys for because if it wasn't for the slave trade, then we wouldn't have anniversaries of its abolition, which would be bad news for people who enjoy *Timewatch*.

Then again, thank goodness that the descendants of the victims of the slave trade started migrating to Britain in the 1950s because quite apart from all their plugging of holes in the labour force and general cultural enrichment of the place, there really is only so long a country can consider Acker Bilk the height of jazz without it becoming embarrassing.

Speaking of the labour force, we've a lot for which to thank the Immigrants who started arriving from the Indian subcontinent in the second half of the twentieth century, not least the introduction of the retail work ethic that led to shops being open when you actually needed them, as opposed to only during the hours when you were at work.[91] Plus, it was mainly through their

---

[91] A work ethic that sadly has yet to translate to the furniture and white-goods delivery industry. I sincerely believe that there should be a law requiring all employees to allow their workers one extra day on top of their statutory holiday rights for staying in to wait for a lorry.

culinary influence that Britain discovered a use for the large numbers of taste buds that it had hitherto not found it necessary to employ.

Mind you, while we're on work ethics, thank the Lord for the Poles, who've actually been here since at least the 1930s, putting up buildings safely and on time. I suppose if we're being fair we ought to doff our hats to all the factory workers and strawberry-pickers and cleaners and farm workers and labourers and bar staff and carpenters and doctors and nurses and God knows what else from all over Europe who come and take up the jobs that need doing. I know I couldn't motivate myself to do it. Some mornings I can barely be bothered to spit out the toothpaste. So perhaps we had better exclude those people from our list, too.

So to be straight about this: it's not the Vikings, or the Normans, or the Jews, or the Lombards, or the Weavers, or the gypsies, or the Huguenots, or the Africans, or the West Indians, or the Asians, or the Poles, or the Lithuanians, or the Bulgarians, or the Turks, or the people fleeing from religious or political persecution, or the white-collar workers from overseas who are here at the behest of their company, or any of that lot.

It's the others. You know the ones. Yes, you do. For example, the . . . Oh.

Anyway, look, it doesn't matter because I've found

someone else to blame. See, we wouldn't even have these vast floods of Immigrants if it weren't for the laws and political set-up of our old nemesis, EUROPE.

EUROPE

Abroad. Funny name for a place, but then it's a funny place. Back in Britain's Golden Age, when Victoria was on the throne, God was in Heaven and fearsome levels of infant mortality, crushing mass poverty and a deadly cholera epidemic were indicators of a country on the up, the purpose of Abroad was very clear. It existed for three specific reasons. In reverse order of importance:

1. To provide the opportunity to travel the world civilising savages by nicking their stuff.

2. To provide the location for books with such titles as *Simkins of the Punjab*, *The Tartar's Snuff Box* or *Congo Ho!*

3. To show us we're best.

In recent times, alas, Abroad has lost its way a bit in the old purpose stakes. Nowadays, we send our own savages round the world for six months once they've done their A levels, not so much to civilise them as to get them out of the bloody house. Inevitably, on their return some of them feel compelled to publish books about their experiences with such titles as *Kraft Singles on a Ghat*, *The Backpack Chronicles* or *Never Buy Second-Hand Ping-Pong Balls in Phuket*. This has the sad effect of showing us, and indeed the rest of the world, that we're no longer best.

Of all the quarters of Abroad that have changed for the worse in recent times, none has done so to quite the extent of Europe. You know Europe – we've all seen it hanging around on maps doing a nice job of framing Britain and making sure that the English Channel doesn't get too wide for charity swimmers. It certainly looks very pretty when you see it on posters of that bridge on kebab-shop walls and behind that woman off *The Sound of Music*. The fact is, however, that the Europe of today is right at the heart of the decline of this country.

Europe hasn't posed us all that many problems over the centuries, really. We've only ever allowed it to invade us twice, once by the Romans and once about a thousand years later by the Normans,[92] and even then that was only because we were interested in

[92] The Vikings don't really count because that was less an invasion and more an aggressively overenthusiastic house move. Plus, they weren't technically European, as Scandinavia had predictably returned a 'no' vote to that in a referendum a few years previously.

mosaics and tapestries – the interior-design fads of their day. Every so often in the intervening centuries we've had to go over there and spend a couple of years explaining a few of the subtler points of international relations with the use of longbows or Lancaster Bombers or football hooligans, and on occasion we've had to set fire to one of their boating parties for breaching the very strict etiquette of the Plymouth Hoe Bowls Association, but on the whole we've left the place alone.

All the more galling, then, that since pretty much the Treaty of Rome was signed wherever it was signed – it doesn't really matter – in 1958, Europe has been doing its best to undermine, absorb and destroy Britain and British identity, and succeeding to a distressing extent. Every single thing that is wrong with this country can be traced back to Europe. Europe has spent half a century systematically whittling away everything we hold dear – from the floods of refugees from the new states coming over here, shaming the middle classes by making them realise how badly they cleaned their own houses before they took on a Lithuanian to do it for under the minimum wage, to the banning of red phoneboxes in case colour-blind people mistake them for green and wrongly imagine themselves to be in Ireland.

Think I'm exaggerating? It's all in the papers – what more proof could you need? Anyone who has spent the last decade keeping an eye on Europe through the British press knows full well that Brussels seems to spend its entire time and billions of pounds of our money[93] thinking up laws that are specifically designed to prevent us expressing our national identity. What about the good old British pint, eh? What about that? All this European legislation forcing us to go metric. It's like they deliberately want us to get rid of one of our national emblems, isn't it? Let us leave aside for a moment the fact that a measure of an alcoholic drink might not be a brilliant national emblem when you compare it to, say, an eagle or a bear or a flaming comet or not having a national emblem at all. And let's leave aside, too, the fact that there's absolutely nothing to stop anyone serving the metric equivalent of a pint. And furthermore, let us leave aside the fact of that being pretty much academic, since European law actually allows a derogation for the UK for pints of beer in pubs. And while we're leaving things aside, let's include in that list the fact that this derogation is an example of Europe legislating flexibly and deliberately in favour of

---

[93] And the money of twenty-six other countries, it's true, but we pay more than them because we pay in pounds and they pay in Euros, which, according to the electronic sign outside the Thomas Cook near my house, aren't worth as much. Plus, I expect we have to pay commission on the exchange rate. Yeah, that'd be about right.

Britain. And finally, let's leave aside the sneaking suspicion that everybody needs to grow up a bit. So. Leaving all those things to one side, you've got to say that if Brussels isn't trying to destroy British culture, then it's doing a very good impression of someone who is. Point made, I think.

Of course, there are scores of other examples of idiotic laws and the fact that almost all of them aren't remotely what we were told by the press is neither here nor there. Sure, it turns out that the story about straight bananas and the one about renaming mince pies and the one about banning the name 'cod' and the one about church bells being made illegal and the one about farmers being forced to tear up hedgerows and about a thousand and one others are basically lies, but that doesn't mean they're not true, does it? Eh? No smoke without fire. Which, is probably another piece of European legislation, I shouldn't wonder.

This country's decline can be directly linked to its loss of confidence, and what has caused this loss of confidence? The destruction of the manufacturing base and the radical repositioning of the employment market? The slow decline in social awareness brought about since the war? Or the fact that Europe wants to ban barmaids wearing busty tops? Even though they don't. I think we all know the answer.

Which isn't to say that we aren't living in a country

in which creativity and carefreeness are stifled by stupid regulations. It's just that they're not coming from Europe; they're coming from THE HEALTH AND SAFETY EXECUTIVE.

THE HEALTH AND SAFETY EXECUTIVE

Before you read this section, would you be so good as to spend a few moments reviewing our safety notice? Thank you. Oh, before you review our safety notice, would you please ensure that you are sitting in the correct position, with your back straight and your feet flat against the floor? Many thanks. Actually, before you sit, would you please ensure that what you are going to sit on is a fully working chair and not, say, a live pig moving at speed or a burning tyre? Super. In fact, before you check the status of the chair, we ought to inform you that you are going to have to demonstrate the requisite level of proficiency in chair-checking. You don't have a City and Guilds in furniture observation (intermediate or above)? Well, that's all right because there'll be a course starting in June; you should fill in this form and apply. And what pen were you thinking of doing that with? A retractable Biro? Are you aware of the damage that thing could do if the top pinged off just as someone had their eye right next to it for some reason? Hmm. I'm not sure you are. Well, no matter;

as soon as you get it sent back from our Stationery Risk-Assessment Centre in Reading, you can fill in the form. There's no point complaining; the sooner you get it sent off, the sooner you'll have it back. Just put your shoes on and go to the postbox. In fact, let's have a look at those shoes . . .

Of course, you can ignore all that. There is no safety notice; the whole paragraph was written simply in the interests of heavy-handed satire[94] and by way of introducing our present subject, the Health and Safety Executive, better known as the HSE since their own legislation forced them to shorten their name so that people didn't get repetitive strain injury typing it out.[95] The Health and Safety Executive is a non-departmental government organisation, and its role can best be described as follows: you know how your liver quietly filters the alcohol out of your system until you reach a point where it suddenly occurs to you that you're not having as much fun as

[94] Although I would draw your attention to the corners of this page, which, being right angles, are on the pointy side.

[95] It is no coincidence that repetitive strain injury itself is now more usually referred to as RSI. Indeed, since people started referring to it as RSI in written documents, the number of actual cases has fallen significantly. To such a degree, in fact, that there have become fewer and fewer occasions on which it is necessary to refer to it at all. This has had the unwelcome consequence that levels of awareness of the condition have fallen to such a low that for clarity it has become necessary to type out 'repetitive strain injury' in full again. Naturally, the number of cases has rocketed.

you remember having a short time ago? Well, the HSE is a little like your liver, except that instead of your system it's SOCIETY in general and instead of alcohol it's canoeing trips.

In principle, health and safety is an excellent idea, built on the foundations of the largely unassailable notion that killing your employees by forcing them to compete in fork-lift slaloms during their lunch-hour is not to be encouraged. There is no doubt that the working day is a whole deal cheerier if you're not being dangled from the roof by a window pole and told to try kicking the pigeon turds out of the guttering with the tip of your brogues. In many respects, the fact that there have been no recorded cases of either of these incidents since the inception of the HSE is to be applauded.

However, the HSE and the culture it has engendered have soured a good idea with overzealousness. For example, remember the joy and spontaneity of childhood? Remember them? Well, it turns out that they were dangerous and have had to be killed. Many of the activities traditionally associated with that golden time are now actively discouraged: children are not to climb trees for fear that they will fall out and injure the teacher below who's filling out a safety assessment; nor are they to play conkers in case one rolls away and germinates, causing more of these problem trees in years to come.

These seem like laughable examples of cotton-wool culture whose only real harm is that they help keep Richard Littlejohn in work, but the HSE's attitude has had three profound and worrying consequences for the State of the World. Firstly, they have made SOCIETY more rapacious. In a world in which most people are interested in accruing as many rights as possible while divesting themselves of anything approaching a responsibility, the HSE have not only legitimised that practice but made it potentially profitable to boot. This is why most ad breaks on the telly now feature commercials for companies with names like Ambulance Chasers 4 You and PullaSickie. co.uk, whose sole purpose is to wheedle footling sums of money for people who can't be trusted not to snort Swarfega or repeatedly smash their clavicle with a claw hammer, if left to their own devices. Inevitably, employers are losing time and money fending off vexatious lawsuits from employees claiming dereliction of duty in not putting up signs to warn that the building has a floor, causing the plaintiff to jar their foot against the carpet and sustain psychological damage.

The second consequence is that SOCIETY has been allowed to become stupider.[96] Where it used to have

[96] That SOCIETY had always been pretty stupid in the first place is repeatedly shown throughout history. Witness, for example, the South Sea Bubble, witch-mania and the result of the 1987 General Election.

to think (at least subconsciously): 'The consequences of my licking the spoon after I've stirred this boiling glue may not be favourable and therefore I should probably, for my own sake, avoid doing it', it now assumes that someone has done all the thinking already and that if that someone hasn't provided a special unlickable spoon, spoon-licking must be safe.

In many respects, this ought to be OK, as the death of the unthinking spoon-licker might be seen as a thoroughly modern sort of natural selection: over time, more and more spoon-lickers would perish, while the thinkers who left the spoon well alone thrived. Thus eventually the species as a whole would progress. Alas, no. What has happened in reality is that yet more time and money have been spent developing non-lickable spoon-effect auto-stir systems that can be operated by recalcitrant chimps. Not only does this ensure the survival of those who would otherwise be licking spoons left, right and centre, but it provides the thinkers in the once-challenging glue-stirring industry with so little stimulation and job satisfaction that they start bringing in their own spoons from home to lick just to end it all. The stupid thrive; the thoughtful perish. In other words, the third consequence of the HSE's attitude is that human evolution is actively being reversed.[97]

---

[97] See also MODERN LABOUR-SAVING DEVICES, p.82.

The HSE, though, is only as good as the people who run it. Unfortunately, the people who run it are the ones who run most of the state's day-to-day business, HAPLESS JUNIOR OFFICIALS.

HAPLESS JUNIOR OFFICIALS

The British love their privacy.[98] So much so, in fact, that if I were to ask you whether you, as a British person, loved your privacy, you would most likely refuse to answer me on the grounds of invasion of privacy. Nothing annoys us more than unsolicited questions that require the giving away of little bits of information about ourselves: 'Is this your car, sir?' 'Have you any idea what speed you were doing?' 'Would you just blow into this, please?' These are precisely the kind of niggling personal enquiries that raise our hackles.[99] So badly do British people react to the revelation of their personal details that it is estimated that every census year up to two and a half million people hide in the lavvy for the duration.[100]

[98] This is why they all live on an island – it stops France listening at the wall with a glass.

[99] In many ways, this is no bad thing, as it is unclear what hackles are for besides raising. If therefore they weren't raised every so often, they'd get no exercise at all and atrophy. And what would we do without hackles?

[100] This means that the population figure that is eventually arrived at is drastically below the real number, a statistical shortfall officially referred to as 'the Census Waste of Human Life'. Ahem.

It is also worth noting that British people are not simply concerned for their own privacy, they are very keen that everybody else maintain theirs. In part this is out of a sense of fairness, but mainly it's because knowing what someone is up to is not nearly so much fun as drunkenly speculating that they're tarting about their house in a bacon-rind thong or that they habitually bellow 'The Internationale' at the point of climax. In many respects, what made the people who lived through the Blitz crossest with the Luftwaffe was that going round clattering the walls off their neighbours' houses was playing merry beggary with the local gossip industry.

Naturally, then, a major contributing factor to the sense of unease and defensiveness that pervades modern life is the perception that we are no longer guardians of our own secrets. To some extent, this is only to be expected in a culture where we are being progressively frightened by our government into accepting biometric ID cards, for which we shall have to queue up for hours in some carpet-tiled Lubyanka so that they can take ear moulds and testicle prints from us. Mainly, though, the fault lies with that group of people who will administer this dystopian process: Hapless Junior Officials.

It's odd: you never see job adverts for Hapless Junior Officials in the *Guardian*'s 'Society' supplement or on Ceefax, but there's clearly quite some market out there.

Perhaps like that of spies, the recruiting process of the Hapless Junior Official does not involve the placing of adverts. After all, if you're looking for someone who can't be arsed to take the CD with the nation's bank details down to the post office so it can go off registered, then you're looking for the kind of person who wouldn't be arsed turning up to the job interview in the first place. Maybe instead the powers that be employ tutors in some of the more disappointing universities to look out for likely recruits. These candidates, once spotted (with their tongue stuck in a Coke can or trying to peel a hot dog), receive a tap on the shoulder, following which they receive a harder tap on the shoulder, then a kidney dig and finally they're just asked outright in an exasperated tone if they fancy being a Hapless Junior Official. And who could say no to low pay and guaranteed negative press coverage?

British bureaucratic culture has changed in recent years in such a way that the influence of Hapless Junior Officials has grown dangerously. Not so long ago, it was only officials of mid-level and above who got to leave laptops positively fizzing with state secrets in the back of unlicensed minicabs on their way home from Poteen Night in the MI6 canteen. Nowadays, in another glorious example of why the democratisation of SOCIETY and technological progress are not necessarily happy bedfellows, it only takes a Hapless Junior Official who hasn't got the wherewithal to think of a word with six letters being put in charge of password-encrypting the disk with the Child Benefit records on and before you know it Kelly from Card Services is ringing you up telling you that you just withdrew £3,000 from an ATM in Kuala Lumpur.[101]

Previously, such sensitive data was protected from being sent through ordinary post by the fact that it was stored on index cards in about three football pitches' worth of mahogany filing cabinets and the Hapless Junior Officials of the time would have had trouble getting those through the franking machine. Thus it was that they had to make do with being slow, obstructive and deeply passive-aggressive in their efforts to wire-wool the shiny lacquer coating off everyone else's lives. The advent of digital technology has given them untold scope to wreak havoc. Their outstanding modern haplessness has effectively sold off Britain's assets to non-British organisations on a scale that must make MRS THATCHER sick with envy. Thanks to their efforts, even as you read this, somewhere in a threateningly foreign land there sits the overlord of an Internet criminal gang[102] who is in possession not only of a CD containing every single one of our bank details – bad enough in itself – but

---

[101] This happened to my wife, who pointed out to the representative of her bank that he had called her at home. There was a short pause and then he promised to reimburse her.

[102] Think Keanu Reeves in *The Matrix* crossed with General Noriega.

another one with our mothers' maiden names and yet another with the names of our favourite pets. No wonder none of us feels safe any longer.

Hapless Junior Officials, though, are merely a symptom of a much wider problem, which is the very shallow well of talent from which employers are able to draw these days. Time was that the meanest ink-splasher in the civil service was educated to PhD level and spoke seven dialects of Ancient Greek. Nowadays, however, you're lucky if they've got their shoes on the right feet and they take their iPod out when they're talking to you. This, alas, is symptomatic of THE YOUTH OF TODAY.

THE YOUTH OF TODAY

And so we come to the Youth of Today. Almost no other group is as to blame for the State of the World as this one – not the POLITICIANS, who actually run the place; not the companies, who specialise in setting the expectations of what they refer to as the 'youth market' and then exploiting the response for financial gain; not the papers,[103] who teach us whom to fear and vilify; not even whoever it was who set the trend for pebble-dashing in the 1970s. No, from that grease-smeared KFC wrapper in the rhododendrons, to that graffito on the bus-stop enumerating Alisha's sexual proclivities and relative availability, to the incipient sense of fear that stalks *Daily Mail* editorials and the country at large, the lion's share of the blame must fall on the thin, acne-besmirched shoulders of the Youth of Today. Of course, it goes without saying that it was never like this in your day.

Time was that the trip home from school would go roughly as follows: young Willoughby would wait for

[103] See NEWS (PRINTED), p.16.

his little sister at the school gate so that he might escort her safely home. Together they would cross the park, the little fellow pointing out chaffinches and poplar trees and various types of cloud formation for the diversion and edification of his sibling, their leisurely pace slowed further according to the number of elderly people to whom they naturally stopped to pay their respects on the way. Eschewing the halloos and entreaties of his fellows getting together a good-natured game of scratch cricket on the playing fields, young Willoughby would lead his sister out on to the road and back to their house, picking up litter all the while. Once inside, and having poured each of them a glass of milk, he would pause only to check the BBC to make sure no war had broken out while he had been at school that he would have to lie about his age to sign up to fight,[104] before retiring to his room to study until suppertime.

These days the routine is somewhat altered. Stopping only to exchange a short but intense burst of filth-drenched invective with his little sister about her choice of velour tracksuit bottoms with 'Sex tits' written across the backside, young Willoughby comes loping out of

---

[104] Worth noting here that you often hear older people say that what this new generation really needs is a good war. But is that true? In many ways, the root of the problem is the previous generations' wars, the memorials of which have given the Youth of Today somewhere to hang out.

the school gates, Kappa hoodie hiding his sallow cheeks and drug-yellowed eyes. Having a couple of minutes to spare while he is urinating on the launderette's back door, he checks that the craft knife he filched from the art storeroom is in his pocket in case the next couple of hours throw up an occasion on which he might need to shiv someone in the intercostals during a dispute over a can of Fanta. Satisfied that he is suitably equipped, he joins his fellow scowling wraiths in the park for their habitual evening of dayglo alcohol, own-brand cigarettes, bicycle theft and pensioner molestation. The party breaks up either just after midnight or when one of them has committed actual bodily harm on another, whichever is the sooner.

Ask the habitual reader of newspapers whether they would rather encounter a) a man with dark skin, a beard and a rucksack on a bus or b) a youth with grey skin, scurf and a mobile phone blaring incomprehensible R & B on a mountain bike and they'd be hard pushed to answer you. For if the spectre of the fundamentalist terrorist is the bogeyman of our present age, then the Youth of Today is the bogeybaby. Much has contributed to the present climate of fear – OIL prices, the buy-to-let market, that weird-looking man who just moved in over the road, global warming[105] – but none of them has had the impact on the nation's psyche to match

---

[105] Although technically, global warming is less about the climate of fear and more about fear of the climate.

that of the present generation of bored teenagers. Everyone, simply *everyone*, is terrified of them. In a country whose denizens would otherwise have very little in common beyond a stock refusal to reappraise their attitude towards the bidet, it is the fear of teenagers that pretty much defines us and keeps us together as a SOCIETY. Teenagers are to us in the early twenty-first century what the Blitz was to Londoners in 1941, or what that bizarre face-eating virus was to the people of Gloucester in the mid-1990s, or what dragons were to hapless villagers in the olden days (and indeed still are in certain parts of the West Country).

You can't fault the Youth of Today for being annoying. That is, after all, their job. Certainly, listening to white teenagers from Harrogate talking like their counterparts in some of the less wonderful parts of Detroit might make you want to look into reintroducing a deluxe selection of intermediate- to advanced-level forms of corporal punishment in the mediaeval style (anything involving wooden cogs or the heating of metal, preferably). And, yes, a moment spent on a bus filled with schoolchildren might make you fear for the future of the English language and wonder when the word 'innit' will make its first appearance in Hansard.[106] But this is supposed to happen; each

[106] 'I put it to the Right Honourable Gentleman Mr Speaker that he has wilfully, deliberately and plainly misled the House, innit?' Followed

generation irritates the last. There was probably a time when 'whizzo', 'All pile on the new squit' and 'Isn't that the purple pip?' would have made any passing adult's ear-clipping hand twitch violently. It's just that back then there wasn't the accompanying fear that the little tykes might fillet your eye with a used syringe if you asked them to desist.

The world has turned upside down. These days, if you were to see the Pied Piper merrily leading children out of the town, you'd be less concerned that you were never going to see the children again and more worried that you'd find the Piper staggering back through the town gates fifteen minutes later, bloody and wild-eyed, muttering something about 'animals' that would be easier to make out if he wasn't carrying most of his teeth in his hand.

Nowhere is safe. Pretty soon, it seems, schools are going to have to take a leaf out of newsagents' books and start putting up signs at the gate: 'No more than two children in uniform allowed in at any one time.'

Still, it's all very well blaming the Youth of Today, but, as anybody with half an appreciation of cliché or the editorial policy of most middle-market tabloids will be only too aware, it's all to do with how they're brought up. In other words, I blame THE PARENTS.

by cries of 'Innit! Innit!' from the backbenches. It'll happen. It's in Revelations. Look it up.

THE PARENTS

Here's a bit of simple but unpleasant maths for you: for every hoodied snit you hurry past hanging around a street corner disappointing the English language and licking the inside corners of a Ginsters packet, there are two sacks of skin filled with below-par chromosomes slopping about the place who are supposed to be calling them in for tea. It's all very well blaming THE YOUTH OF TODAY, but there are twice of many of the Parents who need to be held to account.[107]

It's not all that long ago, at least not geologically speaking, that British parenthood was a pretty simple affair. Each parent had a choice of two roles that they could play and which one they ended up with was

---

[107] Of course, this is arithmetical nonsense, as it presupposes that none of THE YOUTH OF TODAY hanging around street corners has any siblings. This is simply not the case, except in CHINA, where it doesn't count because they're all hanging around street corners setting up multi-million-dollar export businesses. This is why they only have one child each in CHINA – they don't need the insurance policy of having more in case the first one can't help them make up their pension shortfall.

based entirely on class and relative wealth. If you were one of THE RICH, your mother would be a haughty persnicketer with a nice line in disguising her frequent trips to the drawing-room drinks table as a hostessly concern for ice-cube stock levels. You would be introduced to her on the first Christmas Day after your fifth birthday and from that point on she would instruct you in the byzantine ways of etiquette and moral acceptability by means of tutting, withholding affection and reading bits out of the society pages of *Worcestershire Life* in a sarcastic tone of voice. On the rare occasions you encountered your father during his infrequent trips home from the City, where he maintained a showgirl mistress and a portfolio of financial investments in countries with poor human-rights records, he tended to be too busy reading the financial pages, whipping a stable boy for mishandling a hound, or charging out of the house threatening to kill some young man your sister had taken a fancy to, to be safe to interrupt.

If you were one of THE POOR, you would only ever see your mother from the back, as she would be permanently standing at the sink, doing something with potatoes. From this position she would dispense wisdom, warmth, love and directions as to what the older children of the house should do to stop t'bairn from skriking.[108] As soon as the potatoes were done,

---

[108] Poor slang for 'to stop the baby from crying'. In truth, poor people rarely ever spoke like this except for the benefit of visiting novelists.

she would die of emphysema. Your father's work at the tannery would keep him away most of the time, but when he did come home, he'd spend the evenings watching his offspring indulgently from behind his briar pipe, twinkling his eyes and being dignified despite his station in life.

This system, which stood for centuries, gave very clearly defined roles to parents and produced generation after generation of decent, obedient, modest, law-abiding offspring. No longer. The schools are full to the gum-covered ceilings with blade-wielding ne'er-do-wells; our pavements teem with skateboarding remedials denting their skulls on bus-stops. What are the Parents of today up to?

Quite simply, the answer is that they are spoiling their children by refusing to be as detached as olden Parents. Where olden Parents might have left their offspring alone in the nursery for weeks on end to play Ludo and forge their feeling of emotional abandonment into something more useful, like homosexuality or the ability to sit in a muddy Belgian trench for four years, the modern lot will insist on engaging with their children on a one-to-one level by screaming at them in the frozen-food section or going on *The House of Tiny Tearaways*. Naturally enough, this means that the child gets far too much attention and the little mignon becomes spoiled. This sin is compounded by the terrible tendency of today's the Parents to drum into their children the notion that they are 'special', giving the child an inflated sense of importance at a time in their life when their CV looks at best a little thin. The sense that the world revolves round them is thus confirmed in the child and they spend their schooldays refusing to listen to anyone in authority and maintaining a MySpace blog.

Of course, part of the problem with blaming the Parents for THE YOUTH OF TODAY is that those two groups do share a distressingly large number of members. If you were to draw a Venn diagram of two sets, where one set represented THE YOUTH OF TODAY and the other the Parents, then the ∩ intersection of that Venn diagram would have to be explained to all the people in it, because they were off giving birth when the rest of the class covered it in maths. Many of today's the Parents are simply not ready to be parents. While this means that they and their offspring have much in common and there are fewer arguments about whether to watch the news or CBeebies, and while it means that life is considerably cheaper as they can all get into theatres and the opera on concession tickets, these the Parents are often not in a position to give the kind of support and advice their child might need, beyond giving them tips on the best way to get a buggy into the boot of a Little Tykes Cozy Coupé.

Since today's the Parents are so young themselves,

we must look further back along the line of the generations. It is no longer enough to blame the Parents, these days we must blame THE PARENTS' PARENTS.

THE PARENTS' PARENTS

The early evening news bulletins are a depressing affair. Partly this is because of the presence of Natasha Kaplinsky, who is to serious journalism what Princess Diana was to serious royalty, but mainly it's because the whole thing is like some sort of catwalk for the Horsemen of the Apocalypse.[109] According to the Office for National Statistics, two out of every three news programmes contain a report on one variety or another of societal meltdown, during the course of

[109] 'And here comes Pestilence sporting an AIDS epidemic in the African style – very much in vogue for the last few years and showing absolutely no sign whatsoever of going away. A true perennial favourite. Lovely detailing on the batik, there. Famine just behind him wearing something baggy and – heavens! – also in African batik. Obviously Famine's done it in much more of a retro-1980s spirit, but still – little bit of an embarrassing clash, that. Could la Maison d'Horsemen be running short on ideas? And . . . Oh, well, I can't believe this. Here comes War wearing a pair of combat trousers with integrated Kalashnikov- and machete-holders designed to fit an eleven-year-old. Unbelievably, it too is made of African batik. Quite extraordinary. We haven't seen this sort of thing since John Galliano cut the arse out of his jeans and all his models turned out to have the same buttocks on. Completing the quartet, here comes Death in . . . Oh. Black. Of course. That guy hasn't had a new idea in millennia.'

which some late-middle-aged lady will be vox-popped and profess herself of the opinion that parents are to blame for not bringing their kids up right. In my household, this opinion always elicits a response from one or other of the members that involves spitting out a perfectly good mouthful of wild-mushroom risotto and screaming at the television, 'And who brought *them* up, you blathering simpleton?' The answer is, she did. Or at least, her generation did. See, it's all very well blaming THE PARENTS, but much of the responsibility for the State of Things must be laid at the Hush Puppied tootsies of the Parents' Parents.

If you ask me – and I'm going to take the fact of your reading this book as some manner of justification for believing that you did – we spend far too much time worrying about what kind of world we are going to leave behind for our grandchildren and nowhere near enough blaming our own grandparents for the overheated spinning ball of filth of which we are now the curators.

The Parents' Parents of twenty years ago were an impressive bunch, forever defending DEMOCRACY from the yellow-toothed jaws of fascism by cracking impenetrable U-Boat codes and drawing fake stocking seams up the back of their legs with eyeliner. A generation forged of steel and concrete, they defended their children's future against the onslaught of tyranny and then ensured that they didn't go off the rails by inventing the 1950s, a decade so dull that although colour film had long since been in general use, all the footage from that time appears to be in black and white. Alas, the Parents' Parents with which we are now saddled can lay no claim to this sort of pedigree. Where their immediate predecessors speak softly and respectfully of listening to the engines of doodlebugs cutting out overhead and where they were when they heard the news that their brother had been shot in an Arnhem foxhole, today's lot clatter on noisily about listening to the Beatles and where they were when they heard the news that Kennedy had been shot.[110]

Today's the Parents' Parents have taken much and contributed little. They lived off the fat of the post-austerity years. If they weren't twisting the night away in milk bars and ice-cream parlours, and asking what people had got for them to rebel against, they were flitting about on Carnaby Street in Mary Quant mini-clothes trying not to remember anything about the 1960s so that they could prove that they had been there should anybody ask them in subsequent years, or congregating on the Isle of Wight in tie-dye bandanas, rubbing mud all over their breasts and pretending to like Blodwyn Pig.

When it came time to put away childish things, the

[110] And if they can do it on another bloody BBC4 pop-culture retrospective series, they're so much the happier.

Parents' Parents became the first generation for whom homeownership was the norm. They all bought their first house for £200 (and will tell you this apropos of absolutely anything, given half a chance). Now, after four subsequent moves and half a lifetime spent stoking a decades-long house-price frenzy that's made the first day of the Harrods sale look like one of those scenes from a period drama when everyone's dancing a minuet, they shake their heads sadly and bemoan the fact that their daughter simply can't afford to get on the property ladder in spite of being the CEO of a major MULTINATIONAL pharmaceutical concern. When they've finished shaking their heads, they put their house on the market for £750,000 and start trawling THE INTERNET for a pied-à-terre in Aix-en-Provence.

Still, maybe the lady in the vox pop was right. Maybe kids aren't being brought up properly these days. Apparently, there *has* been a breakdown in family life. THE PARENTS are out pursuing careers instead of being at home with THE YOUTH OF TODAY, doing the things they're supposed to do like nurturing them and telling them to put the lid back on the Nutella when they've finished smearing their boyfriend with it. Rather, they're out nurturing their careers, which is still the vox-pop lady's fault because they're having to spend four-fifths of their income on mortgage payments and the taxes that go to fund the Parents' Parents pensions.

On the other hand, the present generation of Parents' Parents have lived through a time of much less moral certainty than would previously have been the case. Where their own parents could use the Church as a lodestar for steering their life's course and bringing up their offspring in a moral environment, the current lot have had to make their own way in a world that God has, if not left, then certainly put up a sign on the door saying, 'Back in five mins.' Perhaps, then, the blame really lies with the decline of ORGANISED RELIGION.

ORGANISED RELIGION

Religion, as many a wiser man than me has remarked, is like a sausage. Every culture has its own version, and while the specific ingredients for each might be slightly different, the finished product is broadly the same. Some are stronger than others, some flabbier, some denser, and some basically unswallowable, and while in the old days you would probably have had to go to a specialist to get hold of some, nowadays any old chancer with a website, a PayPal account and a basic City and Guilds in shovelling meat in a sock can get in on the act.

Organised Religion used to be the rock on which SOCIETY was founded. It provided identity, answers, certainty in the face of a tit of a universe and somewhere appropriate to put that spare steeple that you had hanging around. People were able to go about their daily lives happy in the knowledge that thinking about why they existed or figuring out whether it's wrong to, say, shatter someone's metatarsal with a spirit level in a fit of pique need not cut into their valuable whistling time, as all of that sort of thing had been covered by the forefathers of whatever Organised Religion they happened to have been born into.

For many people, though, those certainties are now long gone. The result of this is the current default position among the populace at large of spiritual confusion, borderline nihilism, a sense of being adrift and a gaping need for collective emotional connection and fulfilment that can apparently only be met by the death of a minor royal or the announcement of an extra bank holiday. What these people really need is for Organised Religion to reach out to them and bring them back in, salving their pain and solving the State of the World, but for decades it has simply not been up to the task. Now, why?

It is something of a cliché to say that Organised Religion has failed to move with the times. Of course it has; it's only natural that something dedicated primarily to the preservation and promulgation of myths that are rooted in the beliefs of primitive Bronze Age peoples would find it hard to move with the times. It's not easy to make something that is thousands of years old look jazzy and hip, and indeed it is often inappropriate to attempt to do so; look what happened when the British Museum tried to engage the kids by giving that mummy an iPod.[111]

---

[111] Let me tell you, you've never seen a properly angry demonstration until you've seen the British Egyptological Society marching through Bloomsbury. My word. You should have read some of those placards. Who knew hieroglyphics could be so graphic?

Even so, Organised Religion has failed to rise to a number of important challenges. Principal among these is its refusal to utilise modern storytelling techniques to deal with the death of its central character.

There are essentially three strategies for coping with this sort of loss. Firstly, you can head off the problem before it happens by building the parts of more peripheral characters and making the whole thing more of an ensemble piece, so that when the central figure does go, the effect is felt less strongly (think George Clooney leaving *ER*, or Grace Archer getting hers in that barn). Secondly, you can devise a fantastical storyline for resurrecting the character (think the opening of Season 6 of *Buffy*), the problem being that you cannot do this more than once unless you are making *Doctor Who*. Lastly, you can call the whole thing to a close and have Jeff Buckley's version of 'Hallelujah' play over a montage (think every third American series on E4). Instead of applying these strategies, Organised Religion has chosen to ignore the fact that God has gone and instead is trying that trick of having all the other characters refer to Him as an off-screen presence, constantly saying things to one another like '. . . and tell God I said, "Hi!"' or 'Hey, God! Could you keep the noise down? I'm trying to evangelise over here.' The problem is that this works well enough if you're doing it on *Neighbours* for a couple of episodes while the casting agent finds yet another actress to play Lucy Robinson, but it's a bit trickier to keep it up for decades when you're running the cornerstone of a civilisation. Naturally enough, people have lost interest and the ratings have suffered terribly. Organised Religion really needs to sit down and spit-ball some ideas.

Here's another problem. As many uncomfortable English people over the age of fifty will be all too aware, modern life is a very touchy-feely affair,[112] and while certain officers of Organised Religion have been very vigorous in their attempts to touch and feel as many of the wider community as time and the need for secrecy allow, the institution as a whole has lost ground by failing to embrace this development. Organised Religion is unfashionably negative. It has a tendency to tell people what they are doing wrong, instead of emphasising what they are doing right. This is no good in a world in which people seek easy justification for their own actions from self-help books with titles like

[112] It was not always like this. Within living memory the expression of any sort of emotion was considered at best a weakness and at worst a compelling case for institutionalisation. By the end of the 1960s, being either touchy *or* feely was tolerated by the coming generations. Sometime in the 1990s, the floodgates opened and suddenly if you weren't touching someone and feeling something else you were, rightly or wrongly, seen as the kind of emotionally stunted individual who most likely could only express themselves through the medium of storing rent boys' body parts in a coolbox under their bed.

The Penis-Driven Life or *Accepting Your Inner Brutal Demagogue*. If it wishes to remain relevant in the modern world, Organised Religion needs to stop being so 'Thou shalt not' and start being a bit more 'Well done, thou.' People These Days need praise mixed in with their criticism. 'So, OK, you committed serial adultery over the same period of months that your frequent absences from home helped propel your thirteen-year-old daughter towards heavy marijuana use, *but* well done for having the generosity to spend the money you were supposed to be saving to pay for two weeks at Sea World on jewellery for those women.' That's the sort of thing we need. Is it any wonder that people are staying away from Organised Religion in droves and that the guy ropes of SOCIETY remain loose?

In many ways, though Organised Religion is at a huge disadvantage nowadays in that its central message of love and tolerance and giving up a day a week for worship and contemplation is not remotely able to compete for attention with, say, pictures of a pregnant girl-band member having a crafty fag outside Champneys. Moral worthiness will never be able to claw back ground against the ever-marching parade of perma-tans and mental illness that is CELEBRITY CULTURE.

CELEBRITY CULTURE

Scene 1

We join our protagonists in the careers room of a large-ish comprehensive school in the mid-1980s.

TEACHER: Now, then, Juliet, have you had any thoughts about what you might like to do after your A levels?

JULIET: I thought I might like to do something to do with smashing the unions, miss.

TEACHER: Yes, I noticed your form teacher's assessment made mention of your interest in current affairs. Well, it's good to have a vocation, Juliet; it's just that I'm sorry to tell you that the unions have been pretty much smashed already.

JULIET: Oh.

TEACHER: Yes. So, any Plan Bs? I've got the results of your psychometric test here and the computer is suggesting that you . . . let's have a look . . . either become a dentist or a milkman. Not sure why those two. Did you express an interest in calcium?

JULIET: No, miss. I don't have much in the way of Plan Bs. I really had set my heart on smashing the unions. I mean, I suppose I've always quite liked the idea of being a doctor, or a research neurologist, or a concert pianist, or an architect. When I was little, I wanted to be an astronaut or a fireman, and I suppose I've always enjoyed designing my own furniture in woodwork, so maybe I could do something with that. Other than those, or possibly making use of my extracurricular interests in fabric design and town-planning, I'm pretty strapped for ideas.

Scene 2

The same room, yesterday.

TEACHER: Now, then, Tanisha, have you had any thoughts about what you might like to do after your A levels?

TANISHA: Eh?

TEACHER: [*Sighs*] Have you had any thoughts about what you might like to do after your A levels, *innit*?

TANISHA: Oh! Yeah, well, I wanna be famous, innit.

TEACHER: Famous?

TANISHA: Innit.

TEACHER: Famous as what?

[*There is a pause.*]

TEACHER: Innit.

TANISHA: Famous as me, innit. Famous famous.

[*There is another pause.*]

TEACHER: Sorry, I was just waiting for— Are you not going to say 'innit'?

TANISHA: Nah.

TEACHER: Well, I—

TANISHA: Innit.

TEACHER: [*To self*] I'm never going to get the hang of this. [*To Tanisha*] Look, Tanisha, you can't just *be* famous. You have to be famous for doing something. So if you want to be famous that much, you might want to think about how you're going to do it.

TANISHA: I could get me tits done, innit.

TEACHER: Oh, God. Look. Right. Let's put to one side for the moment the immense can of worms you've just plunged a Swiss Army knife into. Firstly, no, you couldn't, and secondly, breast implants are not a legitimate career move. So how about we find another way to make you famous? Perhaps you could start learning a musical instrument and see where that takes you. Or apparently you're quite good at science – maybe you could go into some sort of medical research. Perhaps you could even be the one who finds the cure for cancer . . . innit.

TANISHA: What about falling out of taxis with no knickers on, innit?

TEACHER: Again, Tanisha, not really a career as such.

There's no, shall we say, tried and tested formal structure to being famous the way you seem to be thinking of being famous.

TANISHA: There is so, miss, innit. Get your mum to buy you some new boobs for your eighteenth for going down China White's and slapping Ulrika Jonsson in front of the paps on the pavement outside. Get invited to the *TV Quick* Awards at the Dorchester on the back of the coverage in the tabloids and hook up with a children's telly presenter. Go home with him, spike his drink and ransack his house looking for sex tapes he made with a prostitute. Leak one on YouTube. Get in the papers by swearing to stand by him while wearing something people can see your nipples through. Abandon the disgraced presenter. Get your mum to get you new tits again for Christmas. Meet a footballer in the *News of the World* box at the Cheltenham Gold Cup and do him behind the commentary van. Get engaged in the car park. Marry him two months later in a glittering Disney-themed wedding at a Berkshire stately home. Sneak a photographer in from *OK!* and then sue them for £2 million for breach of privacy. Get new tits again on the proceeds. Engage a private eye to follow husband around and a series of high-class call girls as a honey trap. Get him caught fingering one in the toilets at Café de Paris. Get photographed a lot walking about looking shattered wearing grey sweatshirts with the hood pulled up. Drag it out for seven months. Be seen at outside tables of fashionable cafés having tense summit meetings. Ensure the sympathy of the public. Sling him out. Get photographed having the locks changed. Do tearful interview for *Heat* in which you reveal you couldn't shower for two weeks after you threw him out because you'd see the tattoo with his name on you'd had done just above the pubis. Imply some form of mental torture but don't specify. Be seen on girly nights out with other scorned women. Get photographed falling out of cabs with no knickers on. Go to rehab. Publish autobiography with accompanying blurb about how, though only nineteen, you've done enough things for four lifetimes. Get ghost writer to make up childhood. Go on *Celebrity Big Brother*. Deliberately but subtly provoke hot-headed fellow housemate into hurtful outburst by maintaining a relentless, gratingly sunny disposition. Ensure the sympathy of the public. Dedicate win to grandmother. Launch perfume. Get new tits. Marry Ingbert Lempek. Innit.

TEACHER: Lembit Öpik?

TANISHA: Innit.

TEACHER: I see. Tanisha, this is just a lot of nonsense you've got from tabloids and dreadful celebrity gossip mags. There is no such career.

TANISHA: There is, miss. We done it in media. Everyone in the class wants to be famous.

TEACHER: Everyone? Dear God.

TANISHA: Well, everyone except Max. He's gonna do PR, innit. It's perfect for him. He's got this wicked camera on his phone, innit.

Celebrity Culture, though, is basically what happens when popular culture gets drunk and cops off with journalism, and the branch of popular culture that is most likely to slug the Jackie D and drop its knickers is, and ever was, MODERN MUSIC.

MODERN MUSIC

Modern Music is utter bilge and entirely emblematic of the decline in quality, originality and heart that afflicts our popular cultural life, and that's an end to it. If you don't hold with this statement, then come back and reread it in ten years' time, when you will nod your head sadly and sigh your agreement because the plain fact is that not only is Modern Music bringing about the slow dwindling of a once-great art form at this moment in time, it always has been and it always will be. The historical record (as people call what we would normally refer to as 'history' when they're trying to make a point) bears this out.

Henrys VIII and the VII quarrelled when the latter thumped on the former's bedroom door demanding to know what 'that crap you're honking through that crumhorn is'. On being informed through his son's gritted set of pretty unpleasant mediaeval teeth that it was 'Greensleeves', the old king retreated down the stone passage muttering unkindly that it wasn't a patch on 'Sumer Is Icumen In'. Socio-anthropologists working in central Europe have discovered the graves of

Neolithic people who came to mortal blows when one of them drilled an extra hole in the bone flute, thus allowing for the controversial introduction of the note 'Re' to accompany the already-established 'Do'. Even Beethoven was so appalled at some of his more modern work that he spontaneously endeafened[113] himself.

One of the great problems with Modern Music is that by and large it is made by THE YOUTH OF TODAY for THE YOUTH OF TODAY (before being ruthlessly marketed back to them and profited from by the Youth of More Days Ago Than They'd Care to Mention). As such, it is a seething hotbed of counterculture notions, nihilism and generally bad scansion, designed to corrupt the minds and the souls of our young people, and the fact that there is not a shred of sensibly stated evidence to support this claim is neither here nor there. Heaven forefend that we should allow facts to get in the way of the truth. Everyone knows that Modern Music has been instrumental in any number of high-school massacres, teenage self-harm episodes and – worst of all in the eyes of many observers – the shy, faltering acting on of feelings of mutual sexual regard by love-struck adolescents. Also, some of those black T-shirts that bands sell their fans these days make everything else in the wash go blue.

As if it wasn't enough to have THE YOUTH OF TODAY

---

[113] It's a medical term. Don't bother looking it up – it just is.

permanently tuned to 1Xtra or Radio Caroline[114] or whatever they have now, some of them are even stirred to start making Modern Music themselves. Such is the pervasive influence of this devilry that young people are taking guitars and keyboards and what have you, hauling them up to their bedrooms and then sitting in there practising for hours on end. Think what they could be doing with that time instead of learning to understand, appreciate and create music. Obviously, the answer is they'd most likely still be sitting in their bedrooms, only indulging themselves in frantic self-abuse and Googling essays to plagiarise, but the point stands.

Thankfully, as we all know, every single problem affecting THE YOUTH OF TODAY can be solved by the reinstitution of National Service, from the refusal to put DVDs back in their sleeves properly to athlete's foot. The same would be true of the influence of Modern Music. Alas, the problem with it runs much deeper than the enthusiasms of a single generation, threatening the very DEMOCRACY we hold dear and which we're trying very hard to make others hold dear by the somewhat roundabout, left-field route of reducing their countries to states of bloody civil war.

Our statesmen, still feeling the effects of the Modern

---

[114] Radio Caroline – the long-since defunct marine rock 'n' roll station of legend – was recently given a Modern Music makeover and relaunched as AyeAyeTunes. Ahem.

Music of their own salad days, are terribly afflicted by the need to appear – and I can hardly bring myself to type the word – *cool*. The pursuit of cool is at best an astonishing waste of human energy, and that is not a commodity which A-list POLITICIANS ought to be squandering. There is something profoundly depressing about watching a middle-aged world leader, tie loosened and top button undone just like the focus group suggested, getting on down for a carefully scheduled impromptu jamming session with some currently popular musicians, who presumably have something in a security services file that they're keen should not see the light of tabloid, grinning like he's thinking that this beats talking Third World debt with the G8 any day. It seems to indicate a willingness to play fast and loose (and a bit flat and slightly behind the beat) with the dignity of their office.

Winston Churchill – voted, lest we forget, 'Greatest Briton of All Time' by the section of the British populace who couldn't quite see how utterly fatuous the whole exercise was – never behaved like that. He knew a thing or two about gravitas and statesmanship. You'll notice that he did not say in his famous Mansion House speech of 1941, 'This is not the end, it is not the beginning of the end, but it is, perhaps, the end of the beginning. Now watch me chop out some handy axe moves on this mother. Bwaaaaang!'

Similarly, there are no extant contemporaneous

historical records to suggest that once Queen Elizabeth I had explained to a people fearful of the coming Spanish Armada that she had 'the heart and stomach of a king, and a king of England, too', Sir Francis Walsingham wheeled out a clavichord and entreated the assembled to 'watch ma bitch lay down some fun-kay plinkin'.' This is, I feel, significant. Those great statesmen and stateswomen – statestypes, if you will – didn't waste their energies arsing about with Mis-Teeq or Aswad; they channelled the lot into winning the wars in which they were engaged. Tony Blair, a politician at embarrassing pains to point out that he would thoughtfully strum a guitar while cogitating on the world's ills at home (behaviour that is simply not acceptable unless you are 1) sitting in a student flat, 2) drinking a £3 bottle of Cab Sav out of a toothbrush mug or 3) trying to get off with an unattainable girl) didn't even manage to finish the war he helped start before leaving office.

This is a problem that is only going to get worse as download services like iTunes and the increased simplicity of creating and arranging one's own music on home computers makes Modern Music ever more accessible to world leaders. It's easy to envisage a time not that far in the future when almost no wars are seen through at all, as statesmen kick them off, then get distracted and spend all subsequent strategy meetings sitting proudly behind their MacBooks and asking their War Cabinet to 'check this baby out. I did it when the Chancellor was banging on about rationing just before.'

But then, Modern Music is really something that most of us, if we so desired, would never have to encounter except in taxis and as the incidental music accompanying annoying jokey segments on *Newsnight*, were it not for the fact that it's constantly played through the wall by YOUR NEIGHBOURS.

YOUR NEIGHBOURS

Oh, sure, we're governed by corrupted and corruptible charlatans, but you can take that. Yes, the manager of your pension fund did a runner with the money and was last seen negotiating the purchase of Bali for his transsexual lover, Heiko, but that's just one of those things. There's no denying that life was easier when you could nip down to the Co-Op for a packet of Trex and some waffles without ten-year-olds brandishing gimlets demanding your mobile phone every few yards, but that is, relatively speaking, a walk in the park. Certainly it's galling that the increased flooding caused by global warming means you keep having to get that ottoman reupholstered just as the price of flock velvet has gone through the roof, but that is simply one of those things that is sent to try you. Indeed, even the whole SOCIETY-slowly-collapsing-in-on-itself-until-it-begins-to-look-like-one-long-recreation-of-that-bit-in-*2001: A-Space-Odyssey*-where-all-the-monkeys-go-mental thing can be borne. No, what really sticks in your oesophagus, what really boils your soup, what really rings your bell and then runs away and hides behind the bins is Your Neighbours.

Your Neighbours, and Your Neighbours alone, are the single most blameable thing in the whole wide world. They are emblematic – and very probably the cause – of all that is dire about the State of the World. They are the single biggest negative influence on your quality of life. Why must they be like they are? Was it something in their childhood? Do they think Supernanny is supposed to be the baddie on those shows? Have they not heard of planning permission? I mean, the street seemed very nice when you first moved in and the house is lovely, although now you come to think of it, the man who sold it to you did have an odd look in his eye. And you did notice him open his signet ring and pour powder in the cup of tea he offered you, though at the time you just imagined you were seeing things. And in fact he did have Radio 3 on awfully loud and he did keep making 'I'll be right there' gestures at his wife, who was sitting outside, pointedly revving the car.

It's the noise, mainly. How do they find so many ways to make noise? you wonder to yourself. Some of it is only to be expected: the strangulated ululations of the fourteen-year-old girl, something akin to Mariah Carey getting into a hot bath, are perhaps inevitable in an age in which *X-Factor* and its ilk have convinced an entire generation that fame is a consequence of singing and that singing is the art of tunelessly hounding a note up and down the register until it gives in; then there's the relentless, treble-voiced imprecations and profanity that filter through the brickwork as her younger brother urges computer-simulated Nazis to 'Die! Die! Die!'; plus the all-night barbecues every time the thermometer goes above 19 degrees,[115] regularly punctuated with the kind of skull-rattling, rasping laughter that puts the 'orc' into 'raucous' (phonetically speaking, at least); and the weekend afternoons of badly applied power tools and bellowing rows as they continue in their endless quest to do something with the architraving that they saw on *Changing Rooms* in 1998. These, though irksome, are at least fathomable, but they seem to have some talent, some genius even, for devising new methods and means of disturbance. It's one thing, for example, to visit and marvel at the Trevi Fountain. It is another to purchase a special replica that uses self-produced hydroelectric power for continuously playing the theme from *La Dolce Vita*, install it as a water feature next to the summer house and leave it on all night. It is another still to fill it with koi carp, which keep getting stuck in the mechanism, causing the warning klaxon to go off at three in the morning.

[115] Celsius, plainly. The best way to convert this to Fahrenheit, for those who prefer that measurement, is to ask the 1960s.

While we're about it, what about the children? How can they be allowed to behave like that? you wonder. What is that boy doing thwacking a hockey stick against the fence for hours at a time, screaming political slogans? Does he even know what 'Death to the West!' means, anyway? Is the girl hanging around the street corner dressed like that because she's waiting to meet other, equally inappropriately attired friends, or is she hoping to earn a little extra pocket money? Why are they always shouting that most objectionable of all swearwords? Are their parents stupidly tolerant or simply unable to control them? Or have you just got the wrong end of the stick and that's what they've called the dog? That dog. The one that seems to regard the paving slab immediately outside your gate as a sort of last-chance restroom before it goes back in the house.

And who waits until the *News at Ten* has finished to put their glass recycling out, anyway? And is it necessary to throw them in the box a bottle at a time? And it must be against local regulations to have a three-storey dormer, surely. And just because that tree overhanging their garden is yours, it doesn't give them the right to Black & Decker the branches off and then throw the bits over the fence, does it? And just because those blokes in that film built a motor-cycle wall of death in their backyard doesn't mean it's a reasonable thing to do.

No. People are dying, Darfur is in a terrible state, we'll all run out of water in less than a generation, but nothing, *nothing* on this great big, green and blue ball will ever befoul your existence like those inconsiderate boors next door.

But look, this is crazy. Your Neighbours really can't be to blame for the State of the World. They simply don't have the time to make this big a mess, not with all that air-rifle practice in the backyard and clog-dancing in the hallway. There must be a larger group of people at fault here. In fact, now I come to think of it, there is; they're there every time I go out of the house. The ever-present, unstoppable, unthinking menace that is MOTORISTS/CYCLISTS/PEDESTRIANS (DELETE AS APPLICABLE).

MOTORISTS/CYCLISTS/ PEDESTRIANS (DELETE AS APPLICABLE)

Try this thought experiment: before you read any further, just take a couple of moments to jot down a list of the ten things that annoy you most about People These Days. Done that? What have you put down? Rudeness? Tendency to use football as an emotional crutch? Eating crisps behind you very slowly on the train? Thongs? Whatever the other nine on your list, I'll bet the majority of you ended up with something along the lines of the fact that people just don't care any more. This is a sad truth – they just do not care. People These Days are astonishingly self-centred, which was the main theme of an impromptu forty-five-minute speech I gave at my wife's best friend's engagement party the other day.

In part we cannot help this as it is human nature; no other animal is quite so egocentric. You don't believe me? Can you name another species that has written quite so many books about itself? Thought not. Not even dolphins, and they're supposed to be cleverer than us.[116] Even taking that into account, humans have become astonishingly egocentric in recent times and this is eroding our relationships with each other and weakening SOCIETY as a whole. It's a vicious circle, egocentricity: if you spend long enough being the victim of selfish idiocy, you start to give up on being courteous and considerate and go down that route yourself. Nowhere is this more evident than on the roads.

The roads in Great Britain are an unpleasant experience fraught with danger. Some of this is down to the effect on health and taste buds of the mechanically recovered cake-effect snacks you inevitably end up buying at motorway services, but more significantly it's because of the attitude of the people using those roads. Who do I mean? Well, it's obvious, isn't it? It's . . .

(Please pick two of the following and ignore the one that applies to you.)

. . . Motorists, of course. Right, Pedestrians and Cyclists? Motorists' unmatched capacity for egocentrism can be demonstrated by two peculiar modern phenomena. The first is the strange mutation of the use of hazard warning lights. In a simpler age, when cars were made by Austin and driven exclusively by

---

[116] Although, to be fair to dolphins, any endeavours they ever make to break into the field of literature are naturally somewhat hampered by the paper going all soggy.

men in tweed trilbies and string-back gloves, the deployment of hazard warning lights was restricted to instances of breakdown or for the purposes of checking they were working (between having a look at the dipstick and jacking the vehicle up to examine the tyre tread) in preparation for a short trip to get the evening paper. Today's driver seems to imagine that the hazard warning lights are in fact a sort of spare signal that can be used for anything not covered by the other lights. Thus it is that if the ones on the car in front suddenly start flashing, this could mean anything from 'I will be speeding up and slowing down at arrhythmic intervals over the next fifty or so yards, as I can't remember which one of these houses my sister lives in' to 'That was the left I wanted to take back there – check out this handbrake turn.' The fact that the drivers of these cars somehow imagine that whatever happens to be in their heads as they press the red triangle button will be readable from the gentle blinking of two amber lights is an assumption founded on astonishing egocentrism.

The second, and still more aggravating, phenomenon is the current received opinion among motorists concerning speed cameras. To hear these people talk about what are essentially simple labour-saving devices for the police, you might imagine that Amnesty International need to get their priorities straight and spend less time trying to spring tortured Burmese dissidents from Rangoon jails and more time getting Steve off the three points he got for doing 90 miles per hour down a cul-de-sac. They are, according to these appalling morons, simply a 'government revenue-raising exercise'. Indeed they are. They are raising revenue from arseholes. What possible moral objection could you have to speed cameras? 'I can't believe it – I broke the law, I got caught, and now I've got to pay a fine. What the hell is *that* about? I endangered other people's lives with my own reckless behaviour and suddenly *I'm* the one being held to account. Is that the kind of Britain you want to live in?' Yes. It is. You astonishingly self-centred oik.

. . . Cyclists, of course. Right, Motorists and Pedestrians? May the dear Lord help us all, has modern life created any group more self-satisfied and self-justifying than this irksome herd of metal cattle? There is something about electing to cycle about the place in one's daily life that reduces the most thoughtful and upstanding people to the kind of arrogant undergraduate polemicist you'd cheerfully squeeze through some chicken wire with a four-by-four. Cyclists have a very similar mindset to the one adopted by the clergy of the Catholic Church over the centuries, which is to say that so certain are they of their demonstrable moral superiority that they feel it gives them licence to do pretty much what they like. Only, whereas the Catholic clergy lived like gour-mands on a trolley dash round Selfridges food hall and did their best to introduce as many people as possible to what they would cheekily refer to as their 'trouser sacraments', cyclists have taken the Highway Code to be a series of suggestions that might form the opening of an interesting debate over pasta and a decent Chilean Merlot one night rather than, as is in fact the case, a set of rules. Cycling on the pavement has been illegal since the Highways Act of 1835 (Section 72, if you're interested) was passed, but it seems that over 170 years is not long enough for cyclists to grasp this. Hardly surprising, then, that they've had nowhere near enough time to digest the Road Traffic Act of 1988's direction that they must obey all road signs and traffic signals (Section 36).

At least, I assume that this is the problem, because otherwise it only leaves two possibilities: either they are stupid beyond anything we've even seen on the telly or they have taken their green credentials as licence to be the kind of arrogant, self-centred poltroon that you rarely see outside of Tory Conference fringe meetings and student debating societies. I've lost count of the number of times I've seen some colander-wearing clown clattering into a poor bugger on a pedestrian crossing and then screaming at them as though it were their fault in language that would shame a stevedore.

. . . Pedestrians, of course. Right, Cyclists and Motorists? In recent times Pedestrians have adopted the kind of arrogance and carelessness when it comes to road sense that ill befits their status as unprotected masses of soft organic matter in a world filled with speeding metal boxes. Personally, I blame Luke Skywalker for killing the Green Cross Code man.[117] Where once we were taught to see crossing the road as an obstacle to be overcome with patience and good sense, nowadays people seem to view it as some sort of challenge. Perhaps this is down to the increase in traffic on our roads making it harder to find gaps in which to cross or maybe it's because walking the 30 yards to the pelican crossing outside Woolies would burn off too much of the residual fat they've been so carefully building up. Whatever the reason, the result for Motorists and Cyclists is simply terrifying. It's like a zombie movie out there – vacant-faced life forms just stepping out into the carriageway at any moment with no thought or warning. I should imagine if you were looking for somewhere canny to invest your money, then you could do worse than to sink it into a company that makes brake pads because I don't know about anyone else but I go through about a pair a fortnight thanks to these idiots. The problem is exacerbated on a Friday or Saturday night after chucking-out time, when, as far as I can divine from personal experience, many Pedestrians seem to consider a kebab to be some sort of magical protective talisman.

[117] I think that's right, isn't it? It's a long time since I've seen those films.

But can we really blame Motorists/Cyclists/Pedestrians (delete as applicable) for the death of courteousness and consideration in wider SOCIETY? Are they not simply a symptom of the crashing selfishness that bestrides the modern age like a great big metaphor? Yes, they are. So perhaps we ought to look for the source of that selfishness. As it turns out, we don't have to look that far – only as far as wherever it happens to be that MRS THATCHER has parked her madness.

MRS THATCHER

Ah, Mrs Thatcher. Love her or hate her, you just have to hate her. What younger readers or members of THE YOUTH OF TODAY who have accidentally picked up this book in the hope that it is some sort of video game may not realise is that for a good number of people over the age of thirty, the initial reaction to any problem whatsoever is to blame Thatcher. This may seem an odd response, perhaps even dated or irrelevant, but what you have to understand is that it's a habit that is hard to break. Particularly after eleven years' almost daily practice. Seriously. Watch this. The state of the railways? I blame Thatcher. The disastrous general loss of a sense of responsibility towards others? I blame Thatcher. The fact that I can't find the paperwork for my ISA anywhere, even though my wife swears she put it in the file next to the *Charlie and Lola* DVDs? I blame Thatcher. The failure of the English cricketing establishment to consolidate the 2005 Ashes victory in the face of a long injuries list, which exposed a lack of reserve manpower usually available to the national side? I blame Thatcher.

See? Piece of cake. It also always sounds plausible. So much so that nobody batted an eyelid when renowned historian and three-initials-sporter A. J. P. Taylor published a revised edition of his classic text *The Origins of the Second World War* in 1989 containing the new chapter 'Thatcher: the Road to Munich'. To be fair, he'd also added chapters entitled 'What Are Leggings For?' and 'For Sale: P-Reg Maroon Ford Escort, £250 ono' and the consensus was that he'd pretty much lost it by then, but you see what I'm getting at here.

There is no doubt that Mrs Thatcher achieved many things in her political life that were remarkable and worthy of approbation. She became prime minister despite tremendous natural disadvantages: she has a bone structure that gives her the perpetual expression of one who is just about to come to a conclusion about whether or not that smell is coming from the bottom of their shoe, and a posture more normally adopted by someone trying to sneak past a window. Indeed, if you look carefully at some pictures of her, you'll note that she is even a woman (observe the handbag and the skirt: that's how you can tell her from Michael Heseltine).

She did, in fact, fundamentally change the politics of her time. After decades of a broad post-war social-democratic consensus between the Labour and Conservative parties, Mrs Thatcher is credited with reintroducing ideology to politics. By 'ideology' we mean 'half-thought-through notions of socio-economic engineering pursued with the bloody-mindedness of a Viking stag party'. It was essentially like putting one of those people who phone *Any Answers* in charge of the country.

Whatever her personal political achievements, there is much for which Mrs Thatcher must take the blame even now, so long after she was hounded from office. Not least the fact that no sooner had she got the password to Number 10 ('Evening, Officer. You look nice,' if you're interested) than she made her way to the cellar, located the large Bakelite switch marked 'British Industry' and turned it to the 'off' position before using a nearby bust of Lord Palmerston to smash it off the wall. Solving the problem of people having to work in badly paid jobs in a failing economy by getting rid of those jobs was certainly radical, but there is an argument to be made that it was akin to throwing the baby out with the bathwater, before going and getting another baby and throwing that one after the first for good measure, and then turning the taps back on and shouting, 'Bring me more babies!' The result was devastating. There was a point in the mid-1980s when nobody in Liverpool had a job except Derek Hatton and the casts of various Alan Bleasdale dramas explaining that nobody in Liverpool had a job except Derek Hatton. Today, Britain's former industrial heartlands are awash with retail parks and conference centres named after the factories, industries and communities whose guts were kicked out to make way for them. Obviously, that's a rather simplistic statement, but it is tremendously therapeutic to type.

The terrific sleight of hand that Mrs Thatcher (now helpfully renamed Lady Thatcher for the avoidance of confusion) managed to pull off to distract the general populace from the fact that most of them would cheerfully have superglued Bacofoil to her fillings was to make almost everybody in the country imagine they were immensely rich and canny investment whizz kids for about a fortnight in the mid-1980s. This she did by what was called, for convenience's sake, 'privatisation'. The convenience element being that if it had been given the correct term of 'brazenly selling you what you already own', it may not have played so well with the key demographic of slow but essentially thin-skinned people who make up the majority of the electorate, and might not have kicked off quite the frenzy of greed and short-termism that it did. In one of the greatest acts of bare-faced cheek since Nero burnt down Rome and used the insurance money to set up a chain of coffee shops, Mrs Thatcher got the people whose taxes paid for various nationalised utilities to buy them off her. This is somewhat like a door-to-door salesman turning up at your house and trying to sell you the door. People, being people, fell for it in droves.

This single policy was emblematic of and set the tone for the slow dismantling of collectivism and community that the rest of her policies encouraged, and their replacement with the highly self-centred mode of living that persists today. A bit unfair? I refer you to the final sentence of the paragraph before last. There.

Still, much as it runs counter to everything that I was taught to give the old lunatic the benefit of the doubt, might it be that Mrs Thatcher was simply the manifestation of a spirit that was more widely abroad? After all, for every weeping miner, she had two cackling white-van men and an ex-public schoolboy with a job in the City and a semi-erection every time she came on the news. And they voted her in time and again. If we're going to blame anyone here, it really ought to be the idiots who kept returning her to Number 10. There's a name for idiots like that. They're called SOCIETY (See SOCIETY, page 1).

APPENDIX:
You Are Not To Blame –
The Proof

It ought by now to be clear to you that there are many parties on whom it is possible to heap blame for The State of Things. But whilst I have concentrated on elaborating on the culpability of others, it must be said that I have been relatively quiet on the subject of your blamelessness. Please don't feel that I've been avoiding the subject to spare your feelings – it is purely a matter of logistics. The cost in terms of time, effort and resources of researching every potential reader of this book and then writing a section for each of them in a special, individually-published edition to be sent to the bookshop nearest their home is, my publishers insist, prohibitive. Apparently, they need to save money to pay for ghostwriters for the various WAGs and 'high class' prostitutes that they seem to be obsessed by currently. Heigh ho. Therefore, I must offer you the following, imperfect solution: Below you will find a short, multiple choice quiz designed to demontrate your utter innocence with regard to absolutely everything. Answer as honestly as you can and we'll meet back at the bottom when I'll prove to you it's all OK. OK? OK.

The Quiz

1. Your local Member of Parliament becomes suddenly afflicted with an acute case of being dead, forcing a byelection in the constituency in which you live. Do you:

   a) Make sure to keep an eye on local press coverage, carefully consider the views of the candidates by ensuring that you get hold of copies of their campaign literature and attend hustings, asking questions when the opportunity arises;

   b) Find it all a bit of a surprise when someone tells you about it three months after the event;

   c) Stand as the candidate for a major party, playing heavily on the disaffection of local people with politics and promising to shake things up in the Palace of Westminster like a latterday Jimmy Stewart, successfully win the seat and then spend the next three years in parliament trying to get a squash date with your party leader and stealing House of Commons toilet paper to send to old girlfriends?

2. On a trip to the supermarket to buy the ingredients for a risotto you plan to cook in the mistaken belief that it will somehow give you a connection with the voluptuous celebrity chef you saw making it on BBC2 the night before, you notice the bit that tells you the country of origin on the plastic tray of pre-shelled peas says that they come from Kenya. Do you:

   a) Replace the packet on the grounds that you can't justify the food miles;

   b) Sheepishly put it in your basket, resolving to try to plan ahead and be a little more seasonally-minded in terms of food choices in the future;

   c) Run round the supermarket playing 'continental bingo', finally shouting 'House!' six foodstuffs down the line when you discover some dried ham that comes from Argentina, before taking the whole lot home, deciding you're a bit tired to cook after all, slinging the whole lot in the fridge, ordering a pizza and rediscovering it all in the form of a sort of lumpy, purple mush at the bottom of your salad drawer six weeks later?

3. A man is set upon and attacked in front of you in the street. Do you:

   a) Calmly but firmly attempt to intervene, in spite of qualms about your personal safety;

b) Walk past, making apologetic faces at the unfortunate victim and faux-cheerily whistling 'I Was Kaiser Bill's Batman' so as not to appear fearful to his attackers;

c) Scream at your cameraman to start filming and begin to intone an overly alliterative report about local residents living in fear – ensuring that you stand in the left of frame so that when you get the report back to base your editor can add the graphic of a flickknife being plunged progressively further into a body labelled 'Public Confidence' as a way of illustrating the trend in violent crime – as all the while the man flails and gurgles in an attempt to refocus your attention?

4. You are walking down your local high street on a leisurely Saturday afternoon shopping trip when you are hallooed by an ebullient and most likely newly graduated young baggage, wearing the dayglo tunic of a charity salesperson. Do you:

a) Stop and explain politely that you already have a number of charity direct debits set up but that you review them on a regular basis and will bear their charity in mind for next time;

b) Quicken your pace whilst flapping your

    hands and doing an insulting and unconvincing impression of a deaf person;

c) Write a letter to the *Daily Mail* stating that whilst you're all for charity and in fact have knitted several items for the church tombola over the years, you don't appreciate being made to feel guilty about people less fortunate than yourself when you're out shopping and that, whilst you're about it, could you just mention that you're actually completely justified in not buying the Big Issue thank-you very much because those badges the vendors wear look very easily fakeable so how can you be sure that the money isn't going to pay for terrorists or gypsy palaces in Romania, eh?

5. There is a global economic crisis of unprecedented proportions. Do you:

    a) Sit tight;

    b) Run around like a headless chicken putting your savings in a series of building societies and then queueing from five in the morning to take them out again and put them in a different one as your barely-financially-literate reading of the money pages dictates;

   c) Press the secret button under the enormous desk in the office you've been using whilst CEO of a just-failed major investment bank, relax in your chair as it shoots down a velvet-lined pipe to a waiting submarine eight storeys below Wall Street, speed out into the East River and away on the journey to the secret man-made island paradise in the South China Sea you've been having built for the last fifteen years for just such an eventuality?

6. You see a helpless Polar Bear floating past you on a big whack of melted off ice. Do you:

   a) Resolve to have your house properly insulated and look into solar panels in an attempt to redouble your personal efforts in the Fight Against Global Warming;

   b) Realise you fancy a Glacier Mint;

   c) Kill it and speculatively hack into its lifeless carcass with a drill to see if there's any oil in there?

7. A female friend explains to you that after a long period of deliberation and soul-searching she has come to the conclusion that her marriage is over but that, heartbreaking though the situation is, she wants to see it as an opportunity to move on with her life as a wiser and more fully-rounded human

being than she was when she married at the age of 23.
Do you:

    a) Commiserate with her but commend her
       fortitude and cicumspection, observing that
       such an approach certainly justifies her
       view of herself as wise and fully-rounded,
       before offering your services as confidant
       and general support in the months and
       years ahead;

    b) Make sympathetic noises for a while and
       then observe enthusiastically that your
       mate Tony always thought she was a bit
       of all right and he's just left his wife and
       kids, so . . .

    c) Say 'Mm-mmm, you go, girl!'

8. A magazine-reading fellow-commuter notes loudly
to a companion that a well-known actress has been
observed in a Los Angeles restaurant sitting next to
a well-know actor. Do you:

    a) Tut quietly behind your copy of *We Need
       To Talk About Kevin* by Lionel Shriver;

    b) Flick through your copy of Metro to see if
       there are any pictures of the event before
       becoming distracted by the horoscopes;

    c) Squeal and post a status update of Facebook
       about it from your mobile phone, mis-spelling
       every second word and including one of more

of the following character configurations: 'Lol!!!!', 'OMG!!!!!', 'WTF!!!!' or ':-o'?

9. You reach a point in your life at which you feel somehow unfulfilled and perhaps even a little undefined as a person. You begin to wonder if there is something missing either emotionally or intellectually in both your day-to-day existence and your broader set of personal experiences. Do you:

    a) Contact a number of old friends to seek their company and, perhaps, advice, whilst sending off for various prospectuses for courses that will allow you to fulfil your long-held but dormant desire to speak a second language;

    b) Drain the rest of the beer from the pint glass into which you've been directing your maudlin gaze, shake your head vigorously and order the same again;

    c) Get a tattoo?

10. A family from Eastern Europe move into the house next to yours. Do you:

    a) Wait a couple of days for them to get unpacked before going round to introduce yourself and enquire as to whether you can be of any assistance in helping them settle into the local area;

b) Studiously avoid making eye contact for fear that you won't be able to understand their accent and you'll accidentally agree to marry their daughter. Or something;

c) Nail three rolls of razor wire across the top of your shared fence and stand on a chair in your garden playing 'God Save The Queen' on a bugle all the livelong day, denouncing it as 'Political Correctness gone mad' when ordered by the local council to desist?

How Did You Do?

Mostly 'A's: You are blameless. See? Told you. You just carry on with whatever it was you were doing. Gift Aiding a charity donation, perhaps. Maybe painting a disabled parking space on the road outside your house just in case someone needs it. Whatever.

Mostly 'B's: Well, you're certainly not helping matters, but neither are you the problem. You might try to think about what you're doing a little more once in a while, but your brain may be already running at near capacity and there's only so much it's reasonable to ask of someone.

Mostly 'C's: All right. Look. Taken at face value, your anwers seem to indicate not only that you are part of the problem, but very likely solely the problem at that. However, that is only at face value. Consider this: if you read those questions and couldn't see which way answering 'C' was going to take you, then you have the kind of mind which would seem to be incapable of very simple reasoning. This may be a product of nature or nurture, but either that's not your fault is it? It's your PARENTS (see p.161).